Cecil Alec Mace, D.Lit. was, up to his death in 1971, Emeritus Professor of Psychology in the University of London. From 1944 to 1961 he was Professor of Psychology at Birkbeck College. Born at Norwich in 1894 he was educated at the City of Norwich School and Queens' College, Cambridge. From 1922 until 1944 he was a lecturer at Nottingham and St Andrews, and later at Bedford College, London. Throughout his career he combined an interest in philosophy with his interests in psychology. He was President of the Aristotelian Society, President of the Psychological Section of the British Association and of the British Psychological Society and was the founder of the Pelican Psychology series. Besides papers in learned journals and contributions to encyclopaedias, his publications include *The Principles of Logic* (1933), *Incentives: Some Experimental Studies* (1935), *Some Trends in the Philosophy of Mind* (1957) in *British Philosophy in the Mid Century*, a volume of which he was also editor. Professor Mace always showed a particular interest in the application of psychology and philosophy in industry, and wrote and lectured widely on this aspect, besides going to the U.S.A. as one of a Productivity Team studying 'education for management'. As a hobby he described the application of psychology in industry as the only field in which he dug as often and as deep as in his own garden. On his retirement his colleagues and some of his old students combined to write an appreciation of his contributions to psychology and philosophy, *C. A. Mace: A Symposium*, which was published in autumn, 1962.

THE
PSYCHOLOGY OF STUDY

C. A. MACE

PENGUIN BOOKS

Penguin Books Ltd, Harmondsworth, Middlesex, England
Penguin Books, 625 Madison Avenue, New York, New York 10022, U.S.A.
Penguin Books Australia Ltd, Ringwood, Victoria, Australia
Penguin Books Canada Ltd, 2801 John Street, Markham, Ontario, Canada L3R 1B4
Penguin Books (N.Z.) Ltd, 182–190 Wairau Road, Auckland 10, New Zealand

—

First published by Methuen 1932
Revised edition published in Pelican Books 1962
Reprinted 1963, 1964, 1965
Newly revised 1968
Reprinted 1969, 1971, 1973, 1976, 1977

—

—

Made and printed in Great Britain
by C. Nicholls & Company Ltd
Set in Linotype Times

Contents

Introduction

THIS little book had its origin in some talks to adult students in extra-mural classes and to teachers interested in pre-university education. These talks were later expanded into a short course for first year university students and published in Methuen's Monographs of Philosophy and Psychology. It transpired that this book was of use and interest to members of professional organizations such as the Institute of Electrical Engineers. In talks to branches of organizations of this kind foundations were laid for revised editions. Other revisions arose out of the discussions in seminars on 'How to write a thesis' and on 'How to write a report for the Directors of your Company' – the latter arising from the agonized complaints of these directors about the failure of communication in reports received from their research staff.

Accordingly, the book in its present form is intended for a public larger than that to which it was originally addressed. It is now addressed to all who study in any way and to all who may wish to show the outcome of their studies in an essay, an examination script, a thesis, or a research report. If there is a central theme in this book it is that *study is self directed education* – that to study anything is a self directed operation. All education, all learning is to some degree self directed, from the nursery to the end of life. In the civilized world all children are sent to school. Some are later sent to college. Of those who do not follow up their schooling in further formal education many continue self directed studies by listening to broadcasts and reading journals devoted to their hobbies. In the civilized world most people continue to study something in some way as long as they live.

Another theme in this book is that all study is research. or at least all students need to be research-minded. One of the most important developments in recent years has been the organization of research in secondary schools. This should afford a valuable foundation for the research activities of local history and archaeological societies, local naturalists and other societies which have enriched the intellectual life of those who do not attend formal courses of instruction.

In the latest, the 1967, revision of the *Psychology of Study* many passages have been rewritten and expanded to meet queries from readers of the earlier editions. I value these letters not only for the kind expressions of appreciation but also for the attention they have drawn to the passages which called for some restatement. In this edition, too, I have expanded some passages with special regard to the needs of students in technological colleges. I have to acknowledge in this connexion my indebtedness to Mr Don Reid, Principal of the Brixton School of Building, with whose humane and practical philosophy of education I have become acquainted through many lunch hour conversations and which is now accessible to students through his distinguished Presidential Address to the Institute of Structural Engineers.

The target audience to which this book is addressed is indicated by its dedication.

TO ALL STUDENTS

This means: To all who are, in a research-minded way, prepared to share with their teachers the responsibility for directing their own studies.

C. A. MACE

CHAPTER 1

An Outline of Human Nature

Through desire a man seeketh and intermeddleth with all wisdom

— Proverbs xvii, I

THE practical utility of the psychologist as a technical adviser on human problems has been enormously increased by his adoption of the working methods and the guiding concepts of the natural scientist. The earlier successes of the industrial psychologists, for example were due less to their specialized knowledge concerning the working of the human mind than to the application of scientific methods to problems that had previously been tackled merely by rule of thumb. But the growth of specialized knowledge itself has been greatly enhanced by the application in psychology of some good general ideas which for many years have been the current coin of other sciences.

One of the most useful of these ideas is the biological notion of a 'function'. The simplest case is that in which we speak of a particular organ of the body as having a function. It is the function of the eye, we say, to enable us to see. It is the function of a pair of legs to enable us to walk. Sometimes one and the same organ may have more than one function. The human tongue enables man to taste, and so in some degree to distinguish between things that are good to eat and things not so good. It also has the function of enabling men to communicate with one another through speech. Some functions depend upon a number of different organs working together. Sometimes, perhaps more often than not, we have to say that a function is exercised by the organism or the person as a whole. This is usually the case with functions studied by psychologists. It is always the case with the functions involved in the activities of study. Observing things, remembering things, thinking about things, reading books, writing essays or theses, are all activities which may each require the exercise of some organs more than others, but all of these activities are functions of the human organism or person as a whole.

To study something, say history or botany or electronics, is an activity peculiar to man – notwithstanding the fact that research into the ways in which animals learn may help us to understand what happens when schoolchildren, college students, and other human beings study. To deal fully with all the activities involved in study would require a large treatise on human psychology. Fortunately the main contents of such a massive treatise can be quite briefly summarized. Hence the seemingly pretentious title of this chapter. It sets out to give a thumbnail account of 'Man and his Nature', an outline of those parts of his make-up which are relevant to his success when he embarks on a course of study, or takes up as a hobby a study of birds, flowers, space travel, or philosophy. A thumbnail sketch must inevitably be condensed and perhaps rather abstract. If the reader is anxious to get to the main items on the agenda he can skip or skim the rest of this chapter and proceed forthwith to Chapter 2. (Justification for such skipping or skimming is given in Chapter 3.)

Man is an organism, that is an organization or a number of organs which working together produce certain effects. He can, accordingly, be compared with a machine. He is a bit of machinery, a bit of instrumentation, composed of a great variety of more or less specialized instruments or tools. Machines in general can be divided into two classes. One class consists of those which go about their business in complete independence of what is going on around them. The more perfect their insulation the better they do their job. A clock is an instrument of this kind. The less it is affected by the weather the better clock it is. The other class of machine consists of those whose function it is to be as sensitive as possible to some kind of change in their surroundings. A recording barometer is a piece of machinery of this kind. What is a virtue in a clock would be sheer incompetence in a barometer.

The human organism combines some of the features of both these kinds of machines. It is sensitive to a great variety of stimuli – light, sound, changes in temperature, etc. – but it is also equipped with mechanisms which tend to keep certain states constant. It has, so to speak, its own built-in thermostat to keep the body at a suitable temperature and other mechanisms of a similar kind.

These instruments are of three main kinds. First, there are the receiving organs (sense organs) through which the organism is sensitive to heat, light, and other physical and chemical features of the environment. These act as thermometers, telescopes, microscopes, and tape-recorders, to which artificial telescopes, microscopes, etc. serve as supplementary aids to perception. A second group of these built-in instruments are tools with which the organism responds with appropriate actions which tend to preserve the organism or to produce other required effects. These are mainly instruments and tools for movement and manipulation. A human being is essentially a jointed frame, the mobile limbs of which are operated by elastic tissues (the muscles) so as to move either the whole organism itself, or things that the organism can handle, such as bricks and bits of wood, or supplementary artificial tools, such as hammers, saws, scissors or fountain pens. The built-in equipment is in itself an extremely versatile tool kit for operating the many artificial instruments of precision which human ingenuity has devised.

Operating between these two sets of instruments there is a third set through which the 'messages' received from the environment are transmitted to the operative tools, and these messages themselves stored and elaborated in ways which make it possible for the action ultimately performed to take into account past as well as present messages, and often to be of a highly original kind entirely different from anything that has been done before.

This may seem an odd way of describing a human being, and so perhaps it is. And it could be misleading. It becomes increasingly tempting today when more and more machines are being invented which can calculate and solve many kinds of problem. It can be misleading if we consider only the similarities between organisms and artificial machines and ignore the differences.

All instruments have functions and uses, serve purposes, are constructed for some end or ends. The operations they perform are goal-directed, so we ask what is a human being for? What are his ends or goals? As a first approximation to an answer one might say that man, like other organisms, is an instrument for responding appropriately to all kinds of stimulation. Then the question will be asked: 'appropriate' in what way? Most biologists and most psychologists concerned with the behaviour of the sub-human species have been content to say that appropriate responses are those that are conducive to self-preservation and the perpetuation of the species. However adequate this account may be for defining the goals of the behaviour of the sub-human species, and perhaps even the behaviour of man in very primitive societies, it is not good enough for the purposes of defining the goals of man in civilized and cultured societies, and it will be found woefully inadequate for defining the goals of study. Human beings are not really concerned with survival or species perpetuation *as such*. They are concerned with maintaining and improving their standard of life. They do not want just to perpetuate life in their children; they want their children to enjoy a standard of life better than their own. The student wants his studies to contribute to this higher standard of life, to contribute to the enjoyment of living. Hence the powers of perception, memory, and thought, and other powers which the student wishes to cultivate, contribute to the attainment of the goals of study in two ways. They contribute in a utilitarian way: that is to say, contribute by enhancing the efficiency with which practical problems can be solved and life secured. They contribute also to the greater enjoyment of life when life *is* secured, to the appreciation of natural beauty and works of art, to the pleasure of reminiscence, the pleasure of imagination, of creative thought, to the enjoyment of activities of many kinds for their own sake irrespective of their survival value.

An adequate psychology of study requires an adequate understanding of human motivation generally, an adequate account of what we humans ultimately want and why we want what we do.

There are at present no entirely satisfactory answers to these questions. There are however several very promising beginnings to the discovery of answers. Earlier in the present century a systematic account of human motivation was developed by the psychologist William McDougall, who attempted to explain all human behaviour and mental life in terms, first, of a limited number of driving forces, which he called primary 'instincts' or 'propensities', and, secondly, of the modification of these driving forces through experience and learning. His theories were for some years widely accepted, and are still of interest, since they do account in part for the ways in which these motivating forces become canalized into sentiments and 'interests', including the interests which motivate students. McDougall's account of human motivation requires some restatement and amplification in the light of later studies of instinct in animals and even more perhaps through the powerful impact of the so-called 'depth' psychologists such as Freud and Jung. What was most important in his general account of human nature and human motivation is set out in an eloquent passage at the end of Chapter 2 of his *Introduction to Social Psychology:*

We may say, then, that directly or indirectly the instincts are the prime movers of all human activity; by the ... impulsive force of some instinct (or some habit derived from an instinct) every train of thought, however cold or passionless it may seem, is borne along towards its end, and every bodily activity is initiated and sustained. The instinctive impulses determine the ends of all activities and supply the driving power by which all mental activities are sustained; and all the complex intellectual apparatus of the most highly developed mind is but a means towards these ends, is but the instrument by which these impulses seek their satisfactions. ... Take away these instinctive dispositions with their powerful impulse, and the organism would become incapable of activity of any kind; it would be inert and motionless like a wonderful clockwork whose mainspring had been removed or a steam engine whose fires had been drawn. These impulses are the mental forces that maintain and shape all the life of individuals and societies, and in them we are confronted with the central mystery of life and mind and will.*

This is, indeed, a very compressed 'outline of human

An Introduction to Social Psychology (eighteenth edition, 1928).

nature', but it is one which with some changes in phrase or terminology (changes of theoretical rather than of practical importance) could receive the assent of many contemporary psychologists. It is accordingly taken as a basis for discussion in the following chapters of this book.

Let us assume, for the sake of argument:

1. That a useful distinction can be drawn between the instruments or mechanisms of the mind which are used in study and the motivating powers which activate these mechanisms – that the mechanisms are those elements which make it possible to perceive, remember, and think, and that the 'motivating' powers are the forces which activate the processes of observing, recalling, thinking.

2. That the motivating powers which activate the processes of study are not merely general biological needs but are specific curiosities and interests, instigating activities some of which have utilitarian ends, others of which are concerned with the enjoyment of experiences and activities pursued for their own sakes.

3. That improving the efficiency of study (or any other activity) is partly a matter of its motivation and partly a matter of the method of using the mechanisms.

4. That the criteria of efficiency in study (as with any other activity) can be defined in terms of the *degree* to which the goals are attained, the *speed* with which they are attained, and the *economy of effort* with which they are attained.

In the following chapters an attempt will be made to apply these broad and rather abstract principles to the particular ways in which the motivating powers influence the operations of the complex instruments of perceiving, remembering, and thinking.

CHAPTER 2

On Perception and on the Characteristics of a Good Observer

You can lead a man to a lamp-post, but you cannot
make him see it

Old Saw (adapted)

THE good student has a great reverence for books. The
better student is more critical of books. He asks for
their credentials. It is an important advance in student-
ship when the young scholar ceases to say 'But, sir, it
says in the book . . .', having realized not only that there
are questions to which parents do not know the answers
but also that answers in a book can be wrong. As a
vehicle of information no book can be the final court of
appeal. Even an inspired book requires a source of inspiration. Mundane books are either records of fact or
of reflection upon fact. The former draw our attention
to the facts, the latter invite us to reflect upon the facts
for ourselves.

Ideally it might be better if we went to the facts direct,
but the book is a useful instrument for economizing
labour – like a table of logarithms. And, as the mathematician wishes to know how the table is compiled, so
with any book on any subject it is good for us to know
how the author came by his information, and on
occasion to test for ourselves the conclusions he has
drawn. Absolute dependence upon books and other
second-hand sources of information is a necessity in
early education. The reference beyond authority marks a
definite stage in the development of the mind. It is the
beginning of study proper. These remarks do not, of

course, apply to the study of books as literature. In this case the books are themselves the facts.

What happens when someone makes an observation? If we could begin at the very beginning in the study of what happens when a living thing becomes sensibly aware of changes in its environment, we might have to begin with the amoeba, but we do not know what, if anything, an amoeba feels. The development of perception is one of those processes which have to be studied backwards. We can best begin by asking what happens when a human being perceives. When for example he sees a flash of lightning and hears a clap of thunder. The process belongs to the first phase, the receptive phase, in the response of an organism to things in his environment.

In normal visual perception, for example, light impinges on the retina of the observer, on his two retinas, producing a pattern of stimulation corresponding to the pattern of events in the field he is observing (these are patterns in time as well as in space). Impulses in the nervous system are transmitted to certain parts of the brain and then the observer sees the flash of lightning. Similarly with the clap of thunder. Sense organs in the inner ear being stimulated by physical stimuli initiate a series of impulses transmitted to the brain, and at a certain point of time the observer hears the thunder. These processes can be compared with what happens in physical machines which make pictures and records of what is happening around them, with cameras, telephone equipment, 'scanning' devices, etc. There certainly are analogies to be noted; but this is one of the cases in which the differences between organisms and artificial machines are quite as important as the similarities.

An act of perception has in common with the physical processes of making a picture, a representation or a record the following features, among others:

1. It has a certain *content*. The 'content' is simply 'what' appears or is presented to the mind.
2. It has a certain *span*. 'The span' defines 'how much' or how many items are presented to the mind.
3. It takes a certain *time*. That is to say, it occurs at a certain speed.

When we have defined *what* appears, *how much* appears, and *how quickly* it appears we have said what it is important to say about the analogies between processes of perception and the physical processes with which perception has been compared. When we have specified *what* is perceived, *how much* is perceived, and *how quickly* it has been perceived we have indicated some of the chief criteria of efficiency in perception. Some, but not all. We have then to note ways in which human perception differs from mechanical processes, and other criteria of efficiency are discovered, some of which are distinctive criteria of the efficiency of human perception and observation. Observation is motivated perception: it is goal-directed, and the efficiency of a process of observation is essentially a matter of the degree to which the several features of the act of perception contribute to the expedition of the attainment of the goal. This indicates further features which afford criteria other than those suggested above. We must add:

4. That what is perceived is always *organized* and that which is presented can be organized in different ways, some of which are better than others for effective observation.
5. That perception is *selective*, and that some selections are better than others, some more relevant than others, to the end in view.
6. That perceptions or observations vary in *accuracy*, and that different degrees of accuracy are appropriate according to the end in view.

7. That perception can be more or less *objective* and that although all observation requires to be objective in one sense, subjective factors in perception can contribute to good observation.

These criteria of efficiency are not independent. They are all in one way or another consequential to the principle that a good observation is one which contributes to the expeditious attainment of a goal, and its attainment with economy of effort. It is for this reason that a great deal of research is being carried out today for improved dials on dashboards and other displays, road signs and other artificial objects of perception, for those who manipulate motor cars, aeroplanes, or other machines.

To take the several points in turn:

1. *Content.* The question is, in respect of content, what does a good observer perceive? The practical function of perception is to enable the observer to know what is going on around him, so as to adjust his actions accordingly either in the present or in the future. So far as the needs of action are concerned, it does not matter whether what appears in the perceptual field is exactly representative of things as they really are. Provided every difference in appearance corresponds to *some* relevant difference in reality, and provided every relevant difference in reality corresponds to some difference in appearance, action can be appropriately adjusted to the situation. It would be a wonderful thing if perceptual 'appearance' corresponded to 'reality' in this way. Under such conditions every object in the environment would be represented by an object in perceptual ex-experience. Every difference, every relation, between two external objects would be paired by a difference and a relation in the content of perception.

This is not possible. It would require built-in equipment combining the powers of a microscope, a telescope, a camera, and, in fact, every instrument of observation. This, of course, is not practical politics. Nor are such elaborate powers required. The fact that, when occasion demands, the natural powers of observation can be supplemented by instrumental aids meets the situation. In fact the 'limitations' of our powers are a very moderate price to pay for the compensations we enjoy. We sacrifice truth in detail in order to see things as a whole. A microscope is an inadequate instrument with which to find your way about a town. The oustanding merit of normal perceptual function is its versatility for the general purposes of life. For the general purposes of life it is sufficient if we possess very moderate powers of sensory discrimination. For some vocations certain more exacting tests must be imposed. A locomotive driver must not be colour-blind; a colour printer must be endowed with higher powers for the discrimination of hues. In all such special cases the psychologist may devise appropriate mental tests, but for the rest of us the chief requirements are of a different order.

2. *Span*. The span of perception is in part a question of organization. With the best will in the world we cannot perceive all that is there to be perceived. The eagle- or lynx-eyed detective, who 'in a single glance' takes in the whole scene before him, may be left to fiction, where in truth he belongs. Human beings have only a limited span of perception. In a momentary glance we perceive, at best, less than a ten millionth of what is before our eyes. It is sometimes said that the normal man cannot take in in a single glance more than about seven separate items. But the significance of any such statement depends upon what is taken as an item. It may, for example, be itself a well-defined pattern or constellation such as Orion or the Great Bear; and seven such items

would constitute a very fair picture of the sky. But even under the most favourable conditions there are limits to the amount we can perceive. For the present it is sufficient to note that, other things being equal, efficiency of perception varies in proportion to its span.

3. *Speed*. It is important that we should perceive quickly, because quickness of perception favours speed in action and economy of time in acquiring knowledge. When what is perceived is something simple such as a sound or a flash of light, the time required to 'take it in' is negligibly short. Other things being equal, sounds are perceived more quickly than lights because the eye takes longer to generate a visual sensation than the ear takes to generate a sensation of sound.* Among the 'other things' which in fact never are equal there are differences in attention, expectation, and interest. If the eye and the ear are stimulated at the same moment, whether we see or hear first will depend upon the direction of attention. So, too, what is expected will be perceived more quickly than something we are not prepared for. The principle of subjective selection which we shall find to be of very general importance in the ordering of our mental life bears upon the speed of perception in the special form of subjective facilitation.

The speed of perception becomes a matter of greater practical importance in connexion with the perception of complicated things or of simple things under complicated conditions. Our knowledge concerning conditions affecting the speed of perception has been considerably advanced by research (referred to above) into specialized forms of perception such as the reading

* This statement is, of course, concerned with conditions under which the ear and the eye receive simultaneous stimulation. With distant objects sight precedes hearing because of the differences in the relative speeds at which sound and light travel.

and interpretation of dials and displays and signals generally. These studies, however, are mostly concerned with what designers could do to facilitate the speed and accuracy of perception. They deal only incidentally with what the reader of dials, signals, and signs does to increase the speed with which he interprets the signals and signs presented to him. Of greater relevance to the student are studies of the factors which affect the speed of reading printed matter. Some of these will be noted in the following chapters.

4. *Organization.* What is perceived is always in some degree and in some way organized. Objects are seen as having shapes, collections of objects fall into patterns. Some form of organization facilitates perception, as when we see the parts of the moon as the face of the man in the moon. Reorganization of the field can disorganize perception, as when camouflage is used to disrupt the perception of the familiar shapes of buildings.

Good organization which facilitates perception depends partly on objective conditions and partly on subjective conditions. The objective conditions include such factors as the actual geometrical properties of the things perceived. Among the subjective factors are the specific motivations in active search. We are more likely to find the needle in the haystack if we know that we are looking for it. Another important subjective factor is the general disposition or habit of looking for form, as when we try to find the concealed face in a puzzle picture, or when we try to see the contour of a piece of country as shown by the contour lines on a map. The objective factors are in general the concern of those who prepare posters and maps or camouflage buildings. The subjective factors are more under the control of the student observer. The overriding principle for him is that looking *for* is much more efficient than just looking *at*.

5. *Selectivity.* As already noted there are differences between the perceptions of human beings and the recordings of machines in respect of selectivity. Both are selective but they are selective in different ways. The right kind of selectivity is a main requirement in efficient observation. Since we cannot observe everything we must endeavour to observe what is most important. In this matter everything depends upon the principles of selection. This is a matter of training, since the forces that determine spontaneous selection are precisely the forces of distortion and prejudice. These forces are the original propensities of man to which reference has already been made. A propensity is, *inter alia*, a disposition to perceive and attend to certain *general sorts* of things. An interest is, *inter alia*, a disposition to perceive and attend to certain *special* sorts of things. Propensities and interests are among the main forces which determine the movements of attention in the perceptual field. The cat, for example, not only has a disposition to catch mice, it has also a disposition to perceive and attend to mouse-like objects, and to discriminate mouse-like noises in its environment. In the case of the human mind it is less easy to define the propensities which determine the selectivity of perception, since the original proclivities have become endlessly modified, and have assumed the forms of derivative 'interests'. We obtain, however, a general picture of the course of development in this respect if we compare the observational processes of a child, a curio collector, and a scientist. In the case of the child, attention is attracted by what is bright, garish, and sensational. In these features no doubt we approximate to what is primitive in the observational propensities. The collector is quick to notice what is 'curious' or rare. In this case observation presupposes a richer memory and more or less organized experience.

The observation of the scientist is more specifically directed by the consciousness of what is relevant to unsettled points of theory.

6. *Accuracy*. Good observation is, of course, accurate observation, just as good measurement is accurate measurement. But *how accurate* should a measurement or any other observation be? One might be tempted to say 'as accurate as possible', but this is a mistake. Students often waste time and energy in making measurements more accurate than circumstances require. In engineering and in the manufacture of such things as razor blades it is generally essential to measure to a thousandth part of an inch, and it is often desirable to measure more accurately than that. But in making bricks or building houses it would be silly to measure with such refinement. Even in the laboratory sciences it is a mistake to measure or calculate to the fourth place of decimals when one or two places of decimals would serve the purpose in hand. Sometimes indeed it is sufficient to make a well-founded judgement that A is larger than B without attempting to say *how much* larger A is than B. This is especially the case in making preliminary observations which open up new fields of research. Missionaries, explorers, and ordinary globe-trotters may report that they got the impression that members of one tribe were taller, more intelligent, or kindlier than members of another tribe without being able to say how much taller, more intelligent, or kindly the one tribe was than the other. Their 'impressions' serve the purpose of suggesting hypotheses worth testing by more accurate quantitative research. The degree of accuracy required varies with the purpose of the inquiry and with the stage of the inquiry.

7. *Objectivity*. Foremost among the observational virtues is the quality of *objectivity*. If it be too exacting

to demand that every object in the environment should be represented in perceptual experience, we may at least ask that the percipient should not introduce from his own imagination things that are not there. This is a simple requirement, but one surprisingly difficult to satisfy. It seems to be well established that children and primitive men have great difficulty in distinguishing what is actually there to be perceived from what they imagine to be there. In this respect we are all children and primitive men when subjected to the conjurer's wiles. This would not be serious were it only a matter of dealing with deliberate sleight of hand; but Nature is a clever conjurer, too. For this reason the scientific observer needs a long apprenticeship. In the physical sciences there are many mechanical aids to observation, but in many fields of scientific research we are wholly dependent upon natural powers of observation. This is one of the central difficulties in the field of psychical research. The facts are often of a kind that admit of no objective tests and of a kind which are to be observed only under conditions especially favourable to subjective interference. In anthropological research, in the study of animal behaviour, and in many branches of psychology we are at the mercy of the observer who comes with travellers' tales, and with reports in which it is almost impossible to disentangle the nucleus of fact from the penumbra of romantic interpretation. Objectivity, or its absence, is in general a pervading character of mental life. Reliability in observation would seem to be accompanied by reliability in memory and judgement. Conversely, memory is liable to the same distorting influences as the process of perception. So, too, is moral and aesthetic judgement. Even the imagination requires to be protected against subjectivity. The quality of objectivity is the power to view all things – in Spinozistic phrase – *sub specie aeternitatis*, more especially in detachment from their bearing upon our private interests and without regard to the incidental emotions they arouse.

The difficulty of securing objectivity arises chiefly from the fact that in a different though equally important way it is necessary for perception to be subjectively controlled. The idea of 'wishful thinking' is familiar. 'Wishful thinking' is believing mistakenly that things are as we should like them to be. There is also 'wishful remembering', recalling the past, mistakenly, as what we wish the past had been. And there is 'wishful perception', mistakenly seeing and hearing things as we should like things seen and heard to be. William James in his *Principles of Psychology* directs attention to the significance of the case of the hypnotized boy who was asked to say what he saw on a dinner-plate adorned by a reproduction of *The Gleaners* (a picture which contains two upright human figures and one stooping figure). He said that he saw on the plate three bananas, two straight ones and one crooked. It is understandable that a boy whether hypnotized or not would be more interested in bananas than in gleaners. In some degree all observers are like the hypnotized boy. Everyone in some degree tends to see what he would like to see. This significant fact to which James drew attention has been abundantly confirmed by laboratory studies of perception and by the clinical reports of the depth psychologists who have shown that what we perceive is affected not only by conscious wishes but also by wishes of which we may not be conscious.

In view of all the facts that indicate that perception may be distorted by conscious, and unconscious, wishes it may seem odd to say that objectivity in perception may depend on subjective factors. But this can be truly said. Objectivity in observation depends upon the 'subjective' *will to be objective,* upon the kind of motivation characteristic of the scientific observer.

These general considerations point to the broad lines along which the education of the observer must proceed. First, however, we must note a matter of high principle. It was the accepted doctrine of the old-fashioned systems of mind-training that memory is the basis of all the higher functions of the mind, and that remembering in turn depends upon good observation. Hence the first lessons in self-improvement consisted of exercises in perceiving. The pupil was instructed, for example, to take a daily walk, observing with care all that was presented to his eyes, and then upon his return to recall everything that he had seen. Systematic exercises of this kind it was supposed would train the memory and in consequence all the other powers. This system, however, puts the cart before the horse. Perception no doubt precedes the intellect in the order of mental evolution, but when the intellect emerges it transforms every process of the mind, informing with intelligence the process of observation no less than memory.

To ensure efficiency in observation is in part a problem of motivation, and in part a problem of control. To neither problem does mere mechanical exercise offer a direct contribution. The 'powers of perception', such as sensory acuity, span, and so forth, depend upon innate endowment, and cannot be, to any phenomenal extent, developed by exercise or practice. In so far as they are so developed the chief prerequisite is adequate motivation. The motivation of perception is principally a matter of organizing the search for information in the service of propensity, of securing for worthier ends what malice does for the prying nose of gossip. It is sometimes supposed that a specific 'instinct of curiosity' supplies the primary motive in scientific research. But if such an instinct there be, it is found in its purity in the bovine state, and science owes less to this than to many other things. It would seem to be a mistake to attribute every manifestation of curiosity to a single source. Curiosity is an ingredient in each of the propensities alike. For what is curiosity if not a disposition to perceive and attend; and what is attention but the will to know? In point of fact, moreover, we find that scientific inquiry arises from every interest in our nature – from the need for nourishment, from the interests of agression and defence, and from the aversion to disease no less than from any specific instinct that may animate a merely curious mind. There is, in fact, a plethora of motives. The practical problem is one of profitable canalization – of directing 'instinctive' curiosity into appropriate channels.

Failure in observation is in general due to dissipation, a failure in discipline, and restriction. The hall-mark of an inspired observation is its *relevance*. An irrelevant observation by the eye is scarcely more excusable than an irrelevant observation uttered by the tongue. Blank staring is relevant to nothing. What gives relevance to an observation is the presence of a question; a question is the only thing it can be relevant *to*. It is important in observation to know what you are looking for, if only for the purpose of recognizing it when in fact you find it. In the experimental and the observational sciences, an observation is made to settle a point of theory; and the more definite the issue the more specific and planful the observation may be. When Torricelli inverted a tube of mercury, thereby inventing the barometer, and when Florin Périer carried his barometer up the Puy de Dôme to observe the influence of altitude, they did not do these things merely to 'see what would happen'.

They must have had a shrewd idea in advance. Otherwise their conduct would have been eccentric.

Such considerations point to a certain limitation to the value of 'the grand tour', and of travel generally, as a means of education. Mere sight-seeing is undirected and unselective observation. Intelligent travel presupposes knowledge. The value of what is seen does not consist in filling the void of an otherwise vacant mind, but in developing in some specific way something already there – in filling some specific gap in an otherwise knowing mind. As a 'sight' a battlefield is apt to compare unfavourably with a field of corn unsanctified by 'historical associations'. The case is different when the eye is guided by the consciousness of a problem – by some historical puzzle, let us say, concerning military tactics.

So, too, a more profound analysis of the psychology of observation would point to certain educational principles relating to the functions of museums. The guidebooks supplied for the use of the general sightseer require to be supplemented by handbooks for the serious student. Much would be gained if specific regional textbooks could be employed in schools – books in which full advantage were taken of local resources and in which the study of specimens could be subordinated to the development of the background which effective observation presupposes.

Our inquiry into the principles of observation has led us to an apparent paradox. We were led to study observation because the perception of fact is the ultimate source of knowledge and of intellectual activity. But we have found that effective observation is the fruit of experience and of the intellectual life. These apparent paradoxes are very frequent in the study of the mental functions. The mental functions are in general mutually dependent. That is the point of saying that mind exhibits an organic unity. But though everything may depend on everything else, there are certain stragetic points from an educational point of view, points at which something may be done to increase efficiency.

It is on this ground that we must reject the simple theory of observational training based on mechanical exercise of the perceptual function. This is not one of the strategic points. We must begin with spontaneous interest and work through the intelligence. We can encourage observation to be focused rather than diffuse. Our instrument is *the question*. As Bacon pointed out, the progress of science is the result of interrogating Nature, not of staring at her. And 'science' does not progress in abstraction; it progresses in individual minds. We must go to Nature, like an intelligent reporter from the press. He goes to his interview with certain definite questions in his mind. The only room for improvement on this model lies in the nature of the questions we should ask.

CHAPTER 3

On Memorization, on Dealings with Books and Lectures and on Examinations

'It is a momentous fact that the man of modern times has become a book reading animal.'
– Alexander Bain (*Practical Essays*)

ON REMEMBERING IN GENERAL

THE systematic use of observation and of experimental methods in the pursuit of knowledge was one of the later fruits of the Renaissance, but, outside the special sciences, the traditional authority of the book has remained a dominating factor in education. In consequence, the problem which looms largest in the student's mind is the problem of memorization. How can he best retain what he reads in books and what he hears in lectures? Can the psychologist help him?

In the records of the last hundred years of psychological research there is much that is highly relevant to the student's problem. The difficulty is to select what is most important. On a first general survey we find that some of the earliest findings of psychologists, and some of the best attested, are apt to strike us as discouraging. One such finding is that many of the most important qualities of mind upon which success would seem to depend belong to our innate constitution and do not admit of any radical modification. These powers mature in relative independence of our environment and of the educational influence to which we are submitted; they do not benefit, to any striking extent, from exercise or practice. This we have found to be the case with the elementary powers of sensory perception. It is probably true also of the ultimate basis of retention. Such considerations, however, provide no justification for listless and despairing resignation. They should direct our attention to an important practical principle. If we cannot improve our native powers we can at least improve the *use we make of them*.

Moderate ability methodically employed is more productive than greater ability employed in an unmethodical way. The pigmy with a lever and a fulcrum can remove obstacles that would defy a giant. Method is equally important in the use of our mental powers. Even though our powers of memory do not change we can remember more by remembering with method. William James summed up the matter in his breezy, downright, and generalizing way in saying that 'All improvement of memory consists in the improvement of one's habitual methods of recording facts.'* Much progress has been made since James's day in ascertaining more precisely what the proper methods are.

A second somewhat negative discovery of psychologists was the fact that we are endowed not with a single general memory but with a group of specialized memories – a memory for figures, a memory for faces, a memory for historical facts, and so on through an almost endless series. These memories are to a great extent mutually independent, so that if one is trained the rest may remain unaffected. We know now that it is no use learning poetry by heart if our only reason for doing so is to improve our memory. At the most it will only improve our memory for poetry. We shall still forget to keep our appointments and we shall still forget what we read in prose. In the language of the psychologists the effects of training are not 'transferred'; they are relatively 'specific'.

* Cf. *Principles of Psychology*, Vol. I, p. 667.

This, too, may seem rather a depressing fact, but we overlook its cheerful implications. The non-transferability of training is the guarantee of our versatility. If our abilities were so connected that training in one influenced the rest we should find that the influence was frequently one of interference. Learning to use a typewriter would prevent us from playing the piano owing to the very different kinds of 'touch' required in the two contrasted operations. Some transference and some interference does occur, but it is very limited. If there were more transference there would needs be more interference. Having acquired one form of skill we should need to think twice before attempting to acquire another.

Another of the cheerful implications of the non-transference of training is the fact that we can say good-bye to those dreadful exercises devised by certain inhuman monsters for the improvement of our powers of memory. A painful example is cited by James from a work entitled *How to Strengthen the Memory, or the Natural and Scientific Methods of Never Forgetting.** The author describes how he treated 'with partial success' the memory of a person advanced in years. 'The method pursued is to spend two hours daily, one in the morning and one in the evening, in exercising this faculty. The patient is instructed to give the closest attention to all that he learns, so that it shall be impressed upon his mind clearly. He is asked to recall every evening all the facts and experiences of the day, and again the next morning. Every name heard is written down and impressed on his mind clearly, and an effort made to recall it at intervals. Ten names from among public men are ordered to be committed to memory every week. A verse of poetry is to be learned, also a verse from the Bible, daily. He is asked to remember the number of

* By H. M. Holbrook, M.D. Quoted by James, op. cit., Vol. I, p. 668

the page in any book where any interesting fact is recorded.'

James remarks that it is hard to believe that the memory of the poor old gentleman is a bit the better for all this torture except in respect of the particular facts thus wrought into it.

The moral is clear. By whatever means we seek to exercise and improve our memory we should train it in those departments of thought in which it will be most profitably employed. If we wish to perform memory exercises – and such exercises are not without their value – we should employ material from our special subjects of study and material worth remembering for its own sake or for its practical utility.

There is a third respect in which the advance of our knowledge concerning memory has been largely negative, but which, for all that, is none the less important. We have been led progressively to abandon what we may call the photographic theory of retention – another theory based on mechanical analogies. Perhaps no one ever held this view explicitly, but much that has been said and much that has been done in education would seem to presuppose it. The memory was treated as a kind of photographic plate sensitive to impressions rained upon it. It was supposed that these impressions are retained with greater or less fidelity according to the nature and the conditions of the impression and according to the original quality of the plate. In the well-known words of John Locke, 'The pictures drawn in our minds are laid in fading colours; and if not sometimes refreshed, vanish and disappear.' In some of us the mind 'retains the characters drawn upon it like marble, in others like freestone, and in others little better than sand.' In some cases, too, the 'impressions fade and vanish out of the understanding, leaving no more footsteps or remaining characters of themselves than shadows do flying over fields of corn, and the mind is as void of them as if they had never been there.'*

These figurative descriptions are in some respects so apt that we fail to see their misleading implications. What this view so signally fails to explain is the *selectivity* of the mind in its remembering. If we can ascertain the principles which determine this selection we shall have understood what is most important in human memory. An important advance was made when it was suggested that the principle was 'subjective', but for a time psychologists were content with the general principle and they were too much preoccupied with inborn individual differences of capacity. The required stimulus to a more fruitful point of view was supplied by Sigmund Freud, the psycho-analyst, who made the staggering suggestion that we forget because we want to. This in turn invites our acceptance of the corollary that we remember when it suits our purpose – a preposterous proposition, but surprisingly near the truth. A little elaboration and the paradox becomes a platitude.

The necessary correction in principle, and the required details are supplied by the conception of memory as a function, as a constituent function in response to stimulation. As perceptual experience enables us to respond to what is present, so memory enables us to respond to what is past, to respond to what is present in the light of past experience. And as with perception so with memory, the motives of selection are to be found in native propensities and acquired interests. Selection is selection in accordance with purpose. It requires but little supplementary evidence to see that when there is a tendency 'to perceive and attend to' things there is also a

* Locke, *Essay Concerning Human Understanding*, Book II, Chapter 10.

tendency to retain and recall them as occasion demands.

But for the problems of the student, which alone concern us here, we need not trace the streams of human energy to their ultimate sources. We may take as our starting-point those derivative and acquired tendencies known as 'interests' and 'tastes'. How an interest in history, or a taste for algebra is acquired is a long and complicated story. It concerns the teacher rather than the student. For our present purposes we may commence from the interests that are already formed. By these the student should be guided in his studies, for on a wise choice his success will largely depend. Though not infallible, the clue afforded by spontaneous interest is one not to be ignored. It is true that ability may not always be commensurate with inclination, but even great ability will not compensate for the absence of motivation. If we cannot augment our inborn powers, their effectiveness may be considerably increased by the reinforcements of spontaneous interest. This is the more important where talent is not pronounced.

The principle is not so great a concession to human weakness as perhaps it seems. It was James who, contrariwise, advised us to keep alive the faculty of effort by a little gratuitous effort every day, by doing things for no other reason than the fact that we would rather not. This no doubt was good advice, but the choice of studies is not the occasion for its application. The student will find opportunity enough. It requires considerable effort even to follow one's inclinations with consistency to their ultimate objectives. In every course of study, however great its appeal, there is grinding work to do, much that can be learned only by concentrated effort. When every mnemonic device has been exploited there remains much that can be acquired only by drudgery and systematic repetition.

Here – on the organization of drudgery – perhaps more than anywhere, the student seeks the psychologist's advice. Fortunately the psychologist has several useful things to say. 'Mechanical' learning has been fairly thoroughly explored. Perhaps the most important discoveries are those which relate to the appropriate distribution of the periods of study. It has been shown that for most forms of 'learning by heart' the periods of study should be short and distributed over as long a time as possible. For example, let us suppose that a student devotes six hours a week to learning a foreign language, and of this he is prepared to devote two to the more mechanical parts of his task – declensions, irregular verbs, and so forth. Various systems of distributing the work are possible. He might, for instance, concentrate his six language hours into a single day leaving the other days of the week free for other subjects. Alternatively, he might devote an hour each day to his language. In accordance with the general principle cited the latter system would be the more efficient. Within this system there would be various ways in which he might distribute the mechanical and the non-mechanical sections of his weekly task. He could devote the first two days to the former and the remaining four to reading and translation. A more satisfactory procedure would be to divide the mechanical section into periods of twenty minutes, leaving forty minutes each day to the more interesting parts of the work. Twenty to thirty minutes have been found to be a suitable period for purely repetitive learning, but for some purposes the distribution of repetitions may be profitably carried even further. There is much to be said for parcelling the material to be memorized into units which can be tabulated on postcards, these being studied for a few minutes each day. A selection of these cards can be carried in the pocket and revised from time to time at odd moments. This not only eliminates much of the monotony of repetitive study, but also allows revisions to take place at the most favourable times. Acts of revision should be spaced in gradually increasing intervals, roughly intervals of one day, two days, four days, eight days, and so on.

On the matter of sheer repetitive drill there is another principle of the highest importance: *Active repetition is very much more effective than passive repetition.* When a list of items has once been learnt sufficiently for the purpose of immediate recall there are two ways of introducing further repetitions. We may re-read this list; this is passive repetition. We may recall it to mind without reference to the text before forgetting has begun: this is active repetition. It has been found that when acts of reading and acts of recall alternate, i.e. when every reading is followed by an attempt to recall the items, the efficiency of learning and retention is enormously enhanced. There are several reasons why this is the case. One is that the procedure automatically secures the most favourable distribution of attention. The items which prove most difficult to recall receive a special welcome from attention on the subsequent reading and a more favourable impression is secured.

The following analogy may perhaps serve to bring together some of the more important facts of the psychology of learning. There is a remarkable parallel between the function of memory and the function of nutrition and digestion. This is, in fact, suggested by many metaphors of daily speech, but so many are the points of resemblance that we may be tempted to suspect the presence of something more than a mere analogy. Both are processes of assimilation, both are dependent on the stimulus of appetite. In both cases there is a natural rhythm of reception and digestion. In memory, as in nutrition, there is an appropriate 'meal'. Both are liable to the danger of excess. Cramming is a kind of forcible feeding, and the mere 'swot' is an intellectual glutton. In both cases there are inborn and acquired tastes, and there is a certain analogy between the ways in which tastes may be acquired. We shall find, too, that in the mental as well as in the bodily life there are certain principles of dietetics.

Curiosity is the appetite of the mind, and good digestion waits on appetite. Information is more readily retained, as we have seen it is more readily acquired, when it comes in answer to a question. If we ask no questions, experience no curiosity and no perplexities, it is doubtful if we shall ever learn, or if by chance we learn, whether we shall retain. We forget because we do not *effectively* want to know. The only effective want in this connexion is the gnawing pain of unsatisfied curiosity. Such pains are the growing-pains of knowledge. The moral for the student is: *Let your questions come. Try to get them clear – then follow their lead as far as ever they will go. And then ask yourself another question.*

The analogy throws light upon the principle of distributing learning. We do not attempt to consume a meal on Monday which will last us through the week. There is a limit to our immediate capacity. As food requires to be assimilated and built into the system so does knowledge. What has been learned requires consolidation. There is also a process of analysis and re-synthesis in thought which is, so to speak, the metabolism of the mind. Relatively little of what we learn do we need to retain in its original form. Some reorganization is required, some individual synthesis relevant to our private intellectual ends. This, as we shall see, is the first condition of 'originality'.

Perhaps a second analogy will help. There is much

that would tempt us to say that the seat of the memory is not in the mind but in the muscular system. It resides, at least, not so much in the receptive as in the responsive side of our nature. We learn by doing, and we learn by *expressing*. We retain information by making use of it, just as we maintain the strength of our muscles by giving them work to do, and as we retain dexterity by continued dexterous action.

Some form of action or of expression would seem to be essential to unimpaired retention. It seems that good conversationalists and great talkers generally have good memories. It is over-simple to suppose that this is due to the fact that, having good memories, they are well supplied with topics of conversation. The reverse connexion would seem to be involved. What is talked about is more firmly impressed upon the mind. Such men when they read a book immediately discuss it with a friend, thus unconsciously employing the potent principles of active repetition.

One of the best ways of mastering a book, as every teacher knows, is to give a lecture on it. In this fact a special principle is involved. Each of us possesses an active and a passive vocabulary. A man's active vocabulary is constituted by those words he habitually uses in speech and writing. His passive vocabulary is constituted by the words he understands but does not usually employ. Facts expressed in the active vocabulary are more intimately known and more securely retained. Most forms of expression compel us to translate information into the active vocabulary we habitually employ. It is thus embodied into the very texture of our being. This, perhaps, is the ultimate justification of the 'essay paper' and the examination – so far as the latter has a genuine educational function. Criticism of the examination system relates chiefly to its diagnostic function, but properly employed it serves in addition an educational purpose. The latter is seen to best advantage when the student is informed in advance of the contents of the examination papers. For the same reason the student is well advised to prepare answers to examination questions. When the questions are suitably selected, this not only prepares the student for examination, it also ensures more permanent retention.

Disproportionate attention to the receptive as opposed to the expressive functions is probably the commonest fault in students' methods of private study. Relatively too much time is spent in reading and attending lectures and relatively much too little in thinking, writing, and oral expression. At the minimum the latter should receive at least an equal share of the time.

The function of expression in assisting memorization is illustrated by another of James's examples, though James himself seems to have missed its full significance. It is the case of a certain Mr Thurlow Weed, politician and journalist, who records his successful memory training system in the following graphic and impressive narrative:*

My memory was a sieve. I could remember nothing. Dates, names, appointments, faces – everything escaped me. I said to my wife, 'Catherine, I shall never make a successful politician, for I cannot remember, and that is a prime necessity of politicians.' My wife told me I must train my memory. So when I came home that night, I sat down alone and spent fifteen minutes trying silently to recall with accuracy the principal events of the day. I could remember but little at first; now I remember that I could not then recall what I had for breakfast. After a few days' practice I found I could recall more. Events came back to me more minutely, more accurately, and more vividly than at first. After a

* Quoted by James, *Principles of Psychology*, Vol. I, p. 665.

fortnight or so of this, Catherine said, 'Why don't you relate to me the events of the day, instead of recalling them to yourself? It would be interesting, and my interest in it would be a stimulus to you.' Having great respect for my wife's opinion, I began a habit of oral confession, as it were, which was continued for over fifty years. Every night, the last thing before retiring, I told her everything I could remember that had happened to me or about me during the day. I generally recall the dishes I had had for breakfast, dinner, and tea; the people I had seen and what they had said; the editorials I had written on my paper, giving her a brief abstract of them. I mentioned all the letters I had sent and received, and the very language used, as nearly as possible; when I had walked or ridden – I told her everything that had come within my observation. I found I could say my lessons better and better every year, and instead of the practice growing irksome, it became a pleasure to go over again the events of the day. I am indebted to this discipline for a memory of somewhat unusual tenacity, and I recommend the practice to all who wish to store up facts, or expect to have much to do with influencing men.

James himself attributes the successful outcome of this discipline to the fact that Mr Weed, expecting to give his account in the evening, attended better to each incident of the day, named it and conceived it differently, set his mind upon it and in the evening went over it again. 'He had acquired a better method of noting and recording his experiences, but,' says James, 'his physiological retentiveness was not a bit improved.' This account, however, scarcely does justice to the beneficent role of Catherine in supplying the necessary stimulus to *expression*. We may not all be so favourably placed as Mr Weed, but we can all make Catherines of our friends.*

* Better, perhaps, of our casual associates. To acquire a memory of such unusual tenacity we should need to possess even more tenacious friends.

The analogy of nutrition and the analogy of muscular exercise, both in their several ways, are more suggestive and truer to the facts than the analogy of the photographic plate. There is a third analogy which is helpful – the analogy of growth. The growth of knowledge like the evolution of the body and the unfolding of a flower differs in a radical way from the progressive accretion of items characteristic of the construction of the mosaic or the building of a house. This difference was obscured in the old 'psychology of ideas', according to which items of information were acquired one by one and built by association into complex wholes.

The natural order in the acquisition of knowledge is from the vague to the precise, from the rough outline sketch to the detailed picture, from the provisional and inaccurate approximation to the refined and balanced truth. This, too, has its practical implications. It illuminates the rule formulated by psychologists that we should learn things by the 'whole' method rather than by dividing what is to be learnt into sections. The primary application of this principle is to such matters as the learning of poetry. To learn a poem of forty stanzas we should proceed, it is said, by reading it through as a whole, not, as we are naturally inclined to do, by dividing it into sections. The reasons commonly given for this advice are that in the sectional method we form unnecessary and useless associations between the end of each section and the beginning of the same section, whereas relatively feeble associations are formed between the sections. The whole structure when it is assembled remains weak at the joints. This rule of learning by wholes requires qualification in the light of other principles. For example, the central elements in a list of items require more attention and more frequent repetition than those at the two extremes. The process of learning material of this kind has been compared to the process of building a bridge which commences with the two ends that gradually grow and extend until they unite in the middle.

Another reason for learning by wholes is one that applies with great force to meaningful material with a definite plan and structure. It is the principle of conforming to the natural order in the growth of knowledge, to grasp the plan as a whole in outline and then to fill in the details. The general plan provides a rigid frame which binds the parts together as organization binds the elements of the perceptual field. This general procedure is appropriate not only to the purpose of sheer memorization, but also to the process of progressive intellectual apprehension – as in reading a book.

ON READING BOOKS

The very earliest texts on the 'Art of Study' date back to the days when there were very few books to read, and study meant mastering some of the most important of those few books. Students studied these books by copying them out several times and by learning them by heart. Today with so many more books to read the questions are: *How much* to read? *What* to read? *How* to read?

How much? It would be interesting to know how much time readers of various kinds actually spend in reading. One early study,* based on a collection of specially designed 'Reading Diaries', suggested that readers generally spend less time in reading than they would wish, that most reading has to be done in relatively short spells, and that students at universities spend less time in reading than many other readers. This last fact

* 'Reading Habits of Today,' by C. A. Mace, *Adult Education*, Vol. XII No. 1, 1939.

should not be surprising. For the university students study is not just a matter of reading. There are lectures to attend, laboratory work to be done. There is the writing of papers, the writing up of lecture notes and laboratory work. And the reading itself is not just reading. Notes and abstracts have to be made.

What should a student read? If he is not working for an examination he can follow his fancy. The college student is guided by his teacher. Some teachers rattle off a reading list in what might seem a very irresponsible way. If the student attempted to read all the books on the list it would take him several years to get through them. If the complaint is made that the teacher does not indicate which books, which parts of each book are essential the teacher replies, 'Good heavens, my students do not expect to be spoonfed. They are mature enough to exercise their own judgement.' This is perhaps a rather heavy responsibility to fasten on young shoulders.

How to read? Many reading habits formed in early years require correction later. Teaching children to read aloud encourages vocal or sub-vocal articulation. Later skill must be acquired in partly visual reading. Another habit acquired at school is that of beginning with chapter 1 and reading on with care and attention to detail right to the end of the book. Different kinds of books, of course, require to be read or used in different ways. The distinction between books which should be read from beginning to end (like novels) and books of reference (like dictionaries) is familiar enough. What is less widely realized is that many texts, especially 'textbooks', are best treated as books of reference. Alexander Bain in his treatment of the Art of Study laid down as his first maxim *Select a Text book in Chief*. This should be mastered before any other is taken up. 'The pupil must be kept to a single line of thought and never required to comprehend, on the same point, conflicting or varying statements'. Here Bain, in many ways so enlightened a man, defended the didacticism of the nineteenth century. Today most teachers of most subjects would say: 'Have at least two texts.' In few subjects is there just one perfect textbook. In the treatment of the same topic in two textbooks one may be better than the other. When the student is not satisfied with the exposition in one book his next step can well be to look at the exposition in another book. If he is still not satisfied he should discuss the difficulty with a fellow student or put the issue to his teacher. Though different kinds of book require to be used in different ways the following procedure is generally useful. The book should first be read as a whole – as nearly as possible in a single sitting. This yields the required schematic apprehension of the subject and of the plan of exposition. At this stage the student should forgo any attempt to master difficult passages except in so far as may be necessary to follow the general trend of the argument. This first general perusal determines the subsequent course to be adopted. Some books will not need to be read a second time. In others only certain sections will call for further study. Others again will merit a detailed second reading. In the second reading the same general principle should be applied to the chapters individually – each chapter being first re-read as a whole and then submitted to detailed scrutiny. The third reading (received only by the most important sections of the most important books) is perhaps strictly not a case of reading at all. It must be done with paper and pen. This is the stage of précis, comment, and logical analysis. It is in fact a case of writing another book – the student's private critical commentary. This is not merely a matter for the expert, it belongs to every stage of study, in school, in the university, and in private intellectual pursuits. Creative and interpretative reading is the only thing which distinguishes the student's memory of a book from a second and inferior edition of the work itself. Education is something more than the process of taking information from one place to another – from a book to a reader's mind.

A word on 'judicious skimming'. Skimming is rapid selective reading. Two points require attention – the speed and the selectivity. Psychological evidence points on the whole to the conclusion that rapid readers assimilate and retain more than slow readers. The question however is involved, and we must avoid hasty generalization and unintelligent applications. It may at least be said that it is advantageous to avoid subvocal articulation and to acquire the habit of purely visual reading. Articulation (attributed to the bad habit of placing over-emphasis in early years upon reading aloud) retards the rate of reading. But rapid reading must be distinguished from lazy and inattentive reading. No less concentration is required in the first rapid survey of the contents of a book than in the later detailed study.

We may also distinguish between 'skimming' and 'skipping'. In the former just sufficient attention is given to the material to enable us to judge its relevance to the question on which we are seeking information. Care must be taken to prevent the intrinsic interest of the material from diverting our thoughts into irrelevant channels. When relevant passages are reached there will be an inevitable change of tempo and a narrowing of attention.

In recent years courses of instruction in rapid reading have been developed and sponsored largely by the 'top managers' in industry who suffer from the ever increasing burden of the printed documents they receive. The value of these courses awaits confirmation, but there is little doubt that they could be of use especially if they included more general instruction on how to read print, how to skip and skim, how to extract essential points, in short on how to study. The truth is that the student must acquire skills in reading in several different ways. He must acquire skill in rapid reading, in skipping and skimming for getting general impression and for a first evaluation of the less important stuff. He must have skill in reading slowly and with concentration the crucial passages of a difficult text. He must read in very different ways, say one of Shakespeare's sonnets and a passage from Kant's *Critique of Pure Reason*.

ON ATTENDING LECTURES

How much time should a student spend in attending lectures? *What* lectures should he attend? And *how* should a lecture be dealt with? At most colleges the scope for choice is limited. He must in the main be guided by his teachers. But colleges and departments within colleges vary in their systems and many are actively experimenting with new teaching methods. Science teachers often say 'We do not set much store by lectures. We like our students to spend all the time they can in the laboratory.' There are Arts departments in which the teachers say 'We have almost abolished lectures. We have replaced them by seminars.' Other teachers say 'We hope increasingly to replace lectures by "programmed learning".' Students can cooperate with these experiments by noting the methods of instruction which they find most, and which they find least, helpful.

When lectures form an important part of the system the student must exercise his judgement. Some lecturers

– God bless them – conscientiously apply themselves to covering in detail an important part of the syllabus. Their lectures cannot be cut – on a short-term view at least. There are other lecturers who are not concerned much about the syllabus. God bless them too! Their lectures may on a long-term view be the most rewarding, lectures the student will recall with veneration in later life. To such lecturers the student may say: 'Sir, I have a very heavy programme this term. Will you excuse me from attendance at your course?' To which any intelligent and understanding lecturer will reply: 'My dear chap, I do not expect anyone who has not the time, or who is not interested, to attend my lectures. Whether they bear on the syllabus or not you would know better than I. After all it is you who are sitting the examination. I am not, thank Heaven.' There are, too, optional lectures on which the student must exercise his judgement. Most colleges of science and technology nowadays, provide courses in the 'Liberal Arts'. To select from these courses is another matter which requires judgement – and a balancing of short-term against long-term objectives.

And how can a student best deal with lectures? The techniques for extracting information from lectures differ from those for extracting information from books. One important difference between the lecture and the book is that in the former everything depends on the first impression. The principle of working from outline to detail here obviously fails to apply. There are three possible methods in dealing with a lecture. Each has its advocates. At one extreme there is the policy of giving one's whole attention to grasping what is said. No notes are taken. The student trusts entirely to his memory for the retention of what is most important. There can be no doubt that this is an excellent mental discipline. It trains the memory in a way in which it may always be usefully employed. It avoids the inevitable distraction involved in taking notes. When we are writing notes something is bound to be missed and we fail to grasp the structure of the lecture as a whole. At the other extreme there is the policy of attempting to secure a verbatim record. This is, in general, only feasible when the lecture is practically dictated or when the student is a competent stenographer. It has obvious disadvantages.

Most students adopt the intermediate course of 'taking notes', of attempting to make an abstract of the argument while it is in progress. To do this efficiently is an extremely difficult feat. In making a choice between these methods much depends upon the character of the lecture and the style of the lecturer. For most purposes the method to be recommended is the first, qualified by some concession to the third. *Everything depends upon the first impression.* Hence the lecture must receive full and undivided attention.

The college student must discover for himself which policy suits him best and which policy is best having regard to the style of the lecturer. In some cases it will be best to take no notes at all. In others it will be important to note some of the points of the lecturer as nearly as possible in the words of the lecturer himself. In passing from school to college the student must prepare himself for the fact that he may be going to a place in which he will receive the best education in the world by the world's worst teachers. His teachers at school had been trained to teach or had at least taught themselves to teach. At the university hardly any of those who teach will have been trained to teach. Their major preoccupation will be with the advancement of knowledge. They may indeed like lecturing, just because they are bursting to express their new ideas. But they may lecture in a way which has no relation to well-prepared lessons which students have been accustomed to receive. The university teacher may turn his back on the class and excitedly write formulae on the blackboard, all the time rattling out staccato pronouncements which are intended to give the class some clue to what he is so excited about. Or he may give what on the face of it is a polished lecture, but one which takes for granted that the lecturer can take for granted that the class takes for granted all that he takes for granted. To be taught by such teachers is one of the greatest educational privileges in the world. But in the odd forms of communication that occur in the lecture rooms of universities the chief responsibility is at the receiving end. That is why, rather paradoxically, university education is the most advanced form of self-education. The student has to find out for himself the best way of listening to lectures.

Whatever policy be adopted, full notes, scrappy notes, or no notes at all, the most important point of all is that after listening to a lecture the earliest opportunity must be taken to reconstruct the lecture and to check up on what has been said. This brings into play the principle of active repetition. It can be done in a cooperative way. Two students can check their notes against each other's notes.

It goes without saying that the student should have no use whatever for the ordinary lecture notebook. The ideal system is that of the loose-leaf record. This is not a question of detail but one of principle. The record in the ordinary notebook is apt to be at best an inferior reproduction, where what is needed is an individual synthesis. Lecture notes should be amplified through reading, thought, and observation, furnished with illustration, critical comments, references, and extracts from every available relevant source. The final record should improve upon the lecture. In intention the lecture is a stimulus; the student's notebook should record some appropriate response.

The book and the lecture are imperfect teaching instruments. Books being expensive and lectures often tedious, university students increasingly clamour for cyclostyled notes. Some teachers do distribute such notes. Perhaps more could be usefully distributed – but this is not a radical solution of the problem. It would perpetuate the malpractice of putting the main responsibility for communication at the teaching end. It would deprive the student from contact with lively minds and with teachers who get a new idea just before or even during a lecture. It would tend to perpetuate a fault in the traditional system which is pinpointed in the story of the young Scottish student who was reprimanded by an old Scottish professor for not taking notes.

'Mr MacTavish,' the professor said, 'are not my lectures of sufficient interest and importance for you to take notes?'

'But Sir,' young MacTavish replied, 'I have my father's notes of your lectures.'

Some teachers anticipate that books and lectures will increasingly be displaced by 'teaching machines'. A teaching machine is a mechanical device which, *in principle*, could do all that a book does and all that a lecturer does, and do it better. Briefly, a teaching machine is a contrivance which presents in sequence a number of bits of information or ideas in the order in which these bits of information can best be acquired. This is what a book or a course of lectures is intended to do. What the machine does, and what books and lecturers do not, is to check up that one item of information or thought has been taken in before passing to the next item. It has built-in devices through which there is feedback from the student to the teacher, so that the teaching machine 'knows' whether it has or has not got its point across. It asks the student a question. If the student gives the right answer it proceeds to the next item of instruction. If the answer is wrong it goes back and repeats the lesson, before proceeding to the next point. It operates for all the world like the most expensive of all pieces of teaching equipment, the private tutor.

The private tutor can give a piece of information, say that William the Conqueror landed at Hastings in 1066. He then asks his pupil questions, such as:

Who landed at Hastings in 1066?

When did William the Conqueror land?

Where did he land?

If the pupil replies that it was King Canute who landed at Hastings or that William landed at Portsmouth or that he landed in 1866, the tutor repeats the lesson.

'I told you,' he says, 'that *William the Conqueror* landed at *Hastings* in *1066*,' and checks up again.

When the right answers are given he goes on to the next fact.

This is what the machine does which a book or a lecturer lecturing to a class cannot do, and it does it by machinery.

The process might seem to be tedious and long drawn out but there is very persuasive evidence that in the long run teaching and learning time is saved, and that learning through teaching machines is more thorough and can be more interesting. The teacher who puts his lessons into a 'programme' for a teaching machine can have the satisfaction of knowing that his lesson has got across and the pupil has the satisfaction of knowing that he has got his answers right. The construction of teaching machines and the writing of 'programmes' is in course of continuous development and there is little doubt that in the coming years more will be heard of these machines and more use will be made of them. In the colleges of the future there will no doubt be a place both for the inspired teachers who, technically, teach so badly, and for the teaching machines which will relieve them of the drudgery of summarizing the facts which the student can learn from the teaching machines, from textbooks, and from circulated lecture notes.

In the meantime it is not unlikely that those who write textbooks or give lectures will improve their textbooks and their lectures by looking at the principles involved in preparing programmes for teaching machines.

In the meantime, also, while awaiting the development of teaching machines, better textbooks, better lecturers, and more cyclostyled notes, students can improve their habits of study by getting to understand the principles involved in the construction of a teaching machine. What is important in the teaching method is that it applies the principles of automation to the process of teaching. It involves no new principles of psychology or education. It applies some well-known principles most of which have been stated or implied in the earlier pages of this chapter.

ON EXAMINATIONS

The foregoing pages have been in the main concerned with study as a process of self-education. In these notes the general principles previously reviewed will be applied, and on some points expanded, with reference to the special needs of the student preparing for an examination. It will be convenient to consider these principles in relation to four phases of the total process:

(a) Planning and preliminary mental adjustments

(b) Routine study
(c) Revision
(d) The examination itself.

(a) PLANNING AND PRELIMINARY ADJUSTMENTS

One of the most profound and practically important truths that the psychologist reports concerning the human will is that *what we do on any particular occasion depends not so much upon what we think and feel and desire on that occasion itself, but upon what we thought and felt and desired some time, perhaps a very long time, before that occasion.* Our minds, in this respect, are like the familiar barrel organ. The tune that is played on any occasion is determined not when the grinder begins to turn the handle, but when that little preliminary adjustment is made which *sets* the instrument for the desired tune. What we shall have done today has been in like manner determined not exclusively, or even in the main, by today's state of mind, but by those antecedent decisions or moments of indecision of yesterday and the day before. A plan for the future, though it allows of no immediate action, lies in wait for its opportunity and serves to counter all the trivial distractions which may be present when this opportunity occurs. But Hell is paved with vague intentions. Failure in examinations, like failure elsewhere, may be the consequence of setting out to do something without being clear concerning what exactly it is that we are setting out to do. Among the most important of the preliminary adjustments in preparing for an examination are those that conduce to an appropriate distribution of attention over the field of study to be covered. To this end it is well to begin with a general survey of the examination syllabus as a whole, and of the books to be read. The growth of knowledge, it has been observed, proceeds in general from outline to detail, and this fact can be applied with advantage not only to single books and chapters of books but also to the syllabus as a whole.

Preliminary adjustments may also serve to facilitate the maintenance of appropriate working habits and a constant level of attention throughout the available time. Hell, let it be repeated, is paved with vague intentions. Intentions may be vague not only in respect of *what* we mean to do but also in respect of *when* we mean to do it. When I say, however firmly, 'I *must* write that letter,' there is nothing in this volition which determines its expression today rather than tomorrow, or tomorrow rather than next year. Apart from some new and different incentive there is no reason why the intention should be carried out at all. To avoid procrastination *it is essential to incorporate the date of execution in the content of an intention.* Instead of saying merely, 'I must work harder at my Greek,' say, rather, 'I must master such-and-such set of irregular verbs by tomorrow evening.'

The practical upshot of these considerations is that the volitions which control a course of study should be specific, and specific in two respects: *Each should define a particular task, and each should define a time for its execution.*

These volitions collectively will constitute a plan and a programme. Perhaps the chief advantage of the examination system lies in the incentive it supplies in prescribing that a certain total task should be completed by a definite date. The student increases the value of this incentive by reducing the total task to a set of specified assignments, each of which is adjusted to his powers and his natural rate of progress, and each of which has its own date of completion.

(b) ROUTINE STUDY

In consequence of such preliminary adjustments, which, of course, will be made not only at the outset, but throughout the whole course of study, the student will set to work each day with a well-defined objective – an intermediate goal on the road to his ultimate destination. Each defined assignment presents a straightforward problem. Here is a body of information which the student desires to possess, to possess in the sense that he is able to recall it at will. He desires to learn a set of facts, to learn these facts quickly, painlessly, and to learn them once and for all. How can this be done?

Of course, he must not expect too much. He must not try to learn them *too* quickly. He cannot expect to learn them *quite* painlessly, and he cannot expect his knowledge to be *absolutely* permanent. He must be prepared to take his time, to take some pains, and he must be prepared to refresh his memory from time to time of the things he already knows.

In the last resort there are three, and only three, ways in which a fact can be learned:

  (i)   by repetition;

  (ii) by the use of mnemonic devices;

  (iii) by the perception of integrating relations.

To illustrate: Suppose that for some reason it is desired to retain the technical nautical terms for the lights of a ship, to be able to recall at will that *right* is called *starboard* and is indicated by a *green* light; and that *left* is called *port* and is indicated by a *red* light. To learn this the student may use one of the three available methods. He may (1) say to himself, 'RIGHT, STAR-BOARD, GREEN; LEFT, PORT, RED,' and he may say this over and over again. This is the method of repetitive learning, which may be more or less mechanical. He may (2) make use of the mnemonic device of noting that the three longer words, RIGHT, STARBOARD, GREEN, 'go together', and the three shorter words, LEFT, PORT, RED, 'go together'. This is an elementary memory system. Or he may (3) 'study' the connexion between the facts, observing, for example, that 'starboard' is etymologically connected with 'steer-board', and that by reason of human bilateral asymmetry the right-hand side of a primitive vessel would be that from which it would be most naturally steered by the use of an oar. In this last method the facts are built up into a stable system of ideas in virtue of intelligible and self-explanatory relations.

Each method has its place and its distinctive utility. The third method is in general to be preferred. Often it is the quickest, and almost invariably it yields the most stable organization of knowledge. The use of mnemonic systems, as remarked in Chapter 3, is not to be despised. Often, rational connexions are lacking between the items of information which require to be retained, and the use of such *memoria technica* as come readily to hand, will serve to eliminate the drudgery of mechanical repetition. In subjects such as anatomy, for example, these artificial aids to memory continue to be extensively employed. But reliance upon memory systems defeats its own purpose, when the system itself becomes over-elaborate.

But when all other expedients have been exhausted much remains in many subjects which can be committed to memory only by being repeatedly brought to mind. Such repetitive learning, however, need not be entirely mechanical. In fact, it is broadly true to say that the general result of much psychological research concerned with repetitive memorization has been to show that such memorization is the more efficient the less purely repetitive it is. Apart from some of the simplest studies of the earliest school years, there would seem to be very little scope for learning by incantation. The following are three useful principles which have their application within the sphere of repetitive learning:

I. Collections of facts may best be memorized in the larger natural systems in which they are found rather than in the smaller artificial sections into which they may be divided.

This is a restatement of the principles of the 'whole' method as opposed to the 'part' method of learning (cf. pp. 43–4). Wholes may be of very different types. A well constructed poem is a whole. So is the chemist's 'periodic table'. The statement of an argument in support of a theory or in proof of a theorem is a whole in the relevant sense. There are of course limits to the size of the whole to which the principle applies, but here, as elsewhere, the application of general principles must be subject to discretion and intelligence.

II. Periods of repetition should be relatively brief and well distributed.

In repetitive learning the successive repetitions at any one sitting are subject to a law of diminishing returns. The first reading has greater value than the second, and the second greater value than the third. It follows that the utility of the repetitions is enhanced by augmenting the number of separate sittings and by decreasing the number of readings at each.

III. Repetitions should alternate with acts of recall.

This principle has its justification in the fact that it facilitates a favourable distribution of attention in each successive reading, and that it facilitates the process of assimilation. It is probably safe to say that the simplest, the most fundamental and the most paying reforms to be introduced into the normal and untutored methods of study are those that require to be made in the interests of effective assimilation. The most common mistake is to devote relatively too much time to the process of mere reception and relatively too little to the process of assimilation.

It is not enough to read a book or to listen to a lecture. The facts presented need to be built into the structure of the mind. The second phase of the process takes the longer time. This is one reason why repetitions require to be distributed. Even an empty interval between readings is better than no interval at all. But the intervals may be more profitably employed by active recall, by various forms of expression, and by all the mental operations which are summed up by the term 'reflection'. *A safe working rule is to devote at least two units of time to the operation of assimilation to every single unit devoted to reception.* In concrete terms this means that for every hour given to reading or attending lectures at least two hours should be spent in writing essays or otherwise making use of the information gained.

(c) REVISION

If it be true (as some psychologists say) that nothing is ever in strict literalness completely forgotten, it is also true that nothing is wholly free from the ravages of obliviscence. Hence the continuous need for refreshing the mind concerning what is already known.

Two broad principles may serve to guide the student in making provision for this need:

(i) Methods of routine study must be designed to facilitate revision.

(ii) Revision should not be deferred until a later stage in the process of preparation for the examination, but should be distributed throughout the whole course of study.

In general, the methods of taking or recording notes which are best for the main purpose of study, are also those that are best adapted for effective revision. Good notes are those that reduce the presented material to a well-ordered statement of essentials. Such statements will exhibit the form and structure of the information abstracted. One of the most common types of structure is that implicit in a reasoned argument. This case, therefore, may serve to illustrate the general procedure.

When an author sits down to write a book it is because there is some question to which he thinks he knows the answer and for which answer he believes that he can give sufficient reasons. It follows that before the reader can claim to have ascertained the essentials in that book there are three items which require to be abstracted:

(i)   What precisely is the *question* being asked?

(ii) What precisely is the *answer* proposed?

(iii) What precisely are the *grounds* adduced in favour of that answer?

To these items attention may be directed not only in dealing with a book as a whole but also in dealing with the smaller sections into which the book will be naturally divided; for these smaller sections will be concerned with questions which are subordinate to the central contention, with the answers to these subordinate questions and with their grounds.

Earlier (pp. 46–7) it was suggested that important books will require three readings. This statement requires some measure of amplification. On the first reading it was suggested that the reader will skim the book rapidly to discover its general plan. This should at least reveal the central questions under discussion, what answers are proposed and the sort of evidence adduced for the theses maintained.

The second reading will be intensive and selective. It will have been discovered that among the author's aims is the intention to defend some specific answer to some specific question. This is enough to go on. The student will proceed

(a) To formulate this question as clearly and as precisely as he can.

This will be the first important 'note' to be recorded. Often certain subsidiary notes will be required here, e.g., elucidations and definitions of terms, and notes on certain assumptions that are being made, and cross-references to other works in which the same question is discussed.

The next step is

(b) To formulate the answer proposed.

To do this will not always be quite so easy as it might at first seem. Some authors do give definite answers to the questions they discuss, but not infrequently they are content merely to discuss a question without coming to anything more than the most tentative conclusions. In the latter case the reader can note only what possible answers are under consideration. Given, then, that an answer to the question is under consideration, the third step is

(c) To formulate the reasons suggested for supposing this answer to be true.

Often more than one such reason will be given. These should be clearly distinguished and noted as (i) ... (ii) ... (iii) ... etc.

By this time it should begin to be clear exactly where

everything in the author's discussions fits in. Items which do not fall under any of the foregoing heads will probably be found to be illustrative material, references to alternative theories, reasons against such alternatives, or possibly mere digressions. In a well-constructed argument everything will have its place, and in ascertaining its place the reader is enabled to assess its importance. The importance of a statement does not so much reside in its 'intrinsic interest' as in its place in and relevance to some coherent scheme. The central objective in the making of notes is to exhibit this scheme.*

The third reading, so far as it is not telescoped with the second (as in the case of the more experienced reader it almost certainly will be) will pass beyond mere analysis and introduce critical and constructive comment. Arguments must not be allowed to pass unless they are manifestly convincing, and counter arguments should be added to the notes as they occur to mind. Notes so constructed will not only serve the purpose of revision; they will facilitate the transition from mere assimilation to independent constructive and critical thought. And remember that revision gives opportunities for collaboration. Use some fellow-student as a sort of teaching machine. It will help him as much as it helps you.

---

* Some works of outstanding importance have received detailed analysis along the lines here reviewed (cf. the 'Analysis of Locke's Doctrine of Ideas' in his *Essay on Human Understanding*, which is incorporated in many editions of that work, and the *Analytical Digests of Mill's System of Logic*). Current textbooks are similarly treated in the manuals provided for cramming. The intelligent student need not despise the use of such aids to learning. He will use them not, of course, as a substitute for the original works but as a check upon his own methods of abstraction. He should not find it very difficult to improve upon the models thus placed at his disposal.

THE EXAMINATION ITSELF

Reduced to essentials the question with which this chapter has been concerned may be formally stated in the following terms:

Given that an item of information, I, is initially presented to the mind at a time t_1, that it has been recalled by revisions at various times, t_2, t_3 . . . t_n, that there is a subsequent interval t_n to t_x, during which there has been no occasion for this item of information to return to mind, upon what conditions does the revival of I at t_x depend?

The total process is one that comprises three phases:

(i)   the phase of reception and assimilation;
(ii) the phase of retention;
(iii) the phase of revival or recall.

In the first phase occur all those complex operations through which a piece of knowledge comes into the mind and is built into the framework of the mind. It includes both the initial impression at t_1, and the set of revivals at t_2 to t_n (which latter play an important part in the process of assimilation). The second phase is that through which the item of information is unconsciously retained. The third contains the highly distinctive operation of revival, or the return to consciousness of what has been unconsciously retained. Reception, Retention, and Recall are the three 'R's' of memory, the precise control of which would be required by any 'Scientific Method of Never Forgetting'.

By far the majority and by far the most important conditions upon which the recall of I at t_x depend are those that are operative in reception. What is not properly received cannot be adequately retained. Next in importance are those that are operative in the phase of retention. The least important are those that operate at the moment of recall. But though the least important they may be very important indeed. It is tempting to say that after the conditions of reception and retention have produced their effects the fate of I is sealed. According to the nature of these conditions the item of information will either return to mind or fail to return to mind at that crucial t_x in the examination room. But though there is much to make such a statement plausible it is not quite true.

The student may very reasonably ask: Is there *nothing* that I can do at the time of the examination itself which will favour the opportune return to mind of facts that I really know?

The question is reasonable in view of the familiar observation that things that are certainly retained fail to come to mind at the moment when they are required. It is not infrequent for a student to complain that he really knew the answer to an examination question, but that he just failed to think of it at the appropriate time. There are at least a few precautions which may reasonably be expected to decrease the frequency of this calamitous occurrence.

The recall of what is known may be inhibited by fatigue. Hence the unwisdom of too feverish exertions in the last few days preceding the examination. Recall is also adversely affected by the inhibiting emotions. Though it is true that the wings of fear may enable us to clear hurdles which are beyond our normal powers, and that necessity is the parent of recall as well as of invention, it is more commonly the case that flurry and examination nerves may inhibit the more skilled operations of the mind. The deliberate cultivation of a slightly elated, but prevailingly cool and collected, frame of mind offers the best conditions for successful performance in examinations.

The failure to recall what is well known may be in large measure due to a type of over-concentration of attention and consequent restriction to the free play of the mind over the total field of relevant information.

The act of revival has its distinctive conditions. Like the process of assimilation it requires time. Hence the student's first concern in entering the examination room should be to make provision for the maximum possible time to be available for the process of recollection. In a three-hour paper in which there are six questions to be answered, thirty minutes, it might be supposed, is the average time available for the recall of material relevant to each of the questions. In this supposition, although the arithmetic would appear to be unexceptional, the psychology is faulty. *The maximum time is allowed to the process of revival when an initial period is devoted to planning the answers to the* whole *of the paper.*

In this connexion it is of interest to note another respect in which revival may be compared with assimilation. In both, a part of the process is unconscious. As assimilation continues for some time after conscious reception has ceased, so the process which contributes to the recall of information may persist after the active search for this information has been abandoned. It is for this reason that a person's name so frequently comes back to mind some minutes after we have ceased our attempt to recall it. The preliminary preparation of the answers to the whole of the paper sets in motion a process of revival which may still go on after our thoughts have turned to other things. Figuratively, one might say, whilst the conscious mind is concerned with writing down the answer to one question, the unconscious mind is engaged in preparing the answer to the next.

A word, in conclusion, concerning tricks and dodges. On the whole it is best to avoid them. There are, of course, many ingenious ways of suggesting that one knows a great deal more than is in fact the case. There are many styles of window dressing, and many ways of being a plausible rogue in the formal examination as in the other tests of life. But although examiners, on the whole, are simple-minded people, they have had as a rule more experience in defending themselves against these devices than the most practised student has had in employing them.

But to put the matter on somewhat higher ground, is it not more reasonable to regard the examination not as a duel but as a species of cooperation? The examiner is not concerned to expose the bottomless pits of ignorance in the student's mind (however much he may suspect them to be there). He is interested rather in the little hills of erudition which also diversify the scenery of an otherwise even plain. In this he relies in the last resort upon the student to help him. The student can help best not by endeavouring to conceal the pits but by drawing attention with a measure of pardonable pride to the presence of the little hills.

CHAPTER 4

On Originality and Productive Thought

It is one of the curiosities of the psychology of the artist that he is generally trying very hard to do something which has nothing to do with what he actually accomplishes
— Roger Fry (*Vision and Design*)

ON WHAT HAPPENS WHEN WE THINK

PERFECT memorization is not enough. What distinguishes the intelligent student from the dictaphone is that the latter will give a more accurate reproduction of what it has been told. If the student has any compensating merit it lies in being something more than a mere recording machine. Originality, it may be suggested. Or imagination? But neither *mere* originality nor mere imagination is enough. We can achieve a measure of originality merely by being wrong where others happen to be right. We can all think of something new. The difficulty is to think of something that is also true and important. Nor is there great value in imagination as such. Imagination is shown by very young children, by primitive people. It is shown in the delusions of the insane, in all of us when we dream our fantastic dreams. 'Imagination' covers everything from these odd primitive mental processes to the creative activities of great scientists and great artists.

Perhaps a good way into the study of originality, imagination, and creative thinking is to take a brief look at some of the things which may be going on in a man when he is said to be 'thinking'. There are of course very many very different things that he may be doing. He may be indulging in 'idle reverie', or enjoying recollections.

He may be calculating, he may be trying to find the answer to a practical or theoretical problem, he may be having an argument with himself on the pros and cons of some thesis. He may be preparing to write a poem, a novel, or a play. He may be getting ideas for painting a picture.

Idle reverie might seem to be a simple case to begin with, but it may well turn out to be the most difficult to discuss and explain. It is allied to what psychologists call 'free association' but 'free association' means different things in different contexts. In the context of the psychological laboratory, experimental psychologists distinguish between 'free' and 'controlled' or 'constrained' association. In a free association experiment the 'Subject'* of the experiment (the person experimented upon) is instructed, for example, to say when a word is shown to him the first word or idea (any word or idea) that the given word suggests to him. He may, for example, given the word 'chair' reply with the word 'table'. He may on the other hand reply unexpectedly 'snakes' or 'Cape Town', and the experimental psychologist tries to define principles or 'laws' of association which will help to explain why the Subject responds in the way he does. (And there are indeed some interesting and plausible laws relevant to this.) In the 'controlled' or 'constrained' association experiment the Subject is not allowed to respond with any word he likes. He is required to respond to the given word with another word which names something in a prescribed relation to what is named by the word presented – a synonym, its opposite or a species of the genus named by the given word. Such experiments have indeed

* In experimental psychology the 'Subject' of the experiment is the person experimented upon. This use of the term is indicated by the capital S.

contributed to our understanding of what happens when a man thinks.

The expression 'free association' has a rather different meaning in a clinical or therapeutic context. Freud, the founder of psycho-analysis, used 'free association' as a means for exploring the unconscious mind. He required his patients to attend to some idea, such as an item in a dream the patient had reported, and to associate freely to this idea, i.e. to report without any inhibition whatever came into the patient's mind when he reflected on the item in the dream – even if the associations were unethical, unaesthetic, or contrary to the conventions of polite conversation. In this way Freud was able to interpret the dream and discover the unconscious factors behind it. These two rather different kinds of free association techniques were combined in some impressive studies by another of the greater 'depth psychologists', Carl Gustav Jung.

Such laboratory and clinical studies help us to understand what happens in idle reverie. They also help us to understand what happens in reminiscence, in remembering and forgetting generally, and what happens, indeed, whenever or however we think.

Some quite general well-established findings may be noted:

1. *That there are causal laws or principles in accordance with which one thought follows another.* When, for example, the idea of lightning suggests the idea of thunder, the sequence is as rigidly determined as the physical sequence from lightning to thunder. This is the case whatever the sequence may be. The laws must help to account not only for the matter-of-fact way of thinking (lightning-thunder). They must also help to account for poetic ways of thinking (the gods with their thunderbolts), for fanciful ways of thinking (that the earth is a

kind of sparking plug), and for eccentric ways of thinking (as when lightning suggests, say, 'gout' or '9 as the
square root of 81'). 'Laws of association' can give not
implausible accounts of why any idea can suggest any
other idea whatever. This indeed is one reason why as
traditionally stated these 'laws' have a dubious scientific standing. They need to be amplified and refined in
ways which explain why the sequence of thought and the
direction of thought differs from one person to another
and in the same person at different times.

2. *That the difference in the sequence of ideas and the
direction of thought under different circumstances is
largely a matter of the 'controls', not only the controls
of controlled association but the similar controls which
operate in all forms of thinking.* There are no associations which are completely free. The distinction is
relative. When, for example, in some verbal game or
trick the opening move is 'Think of a number' and this
is followed by 'Double it', the response to the first
instruction is *relatively* free and the response to the
second more constrained. The first instruction restricts
the association to numbers. The second instruction does
not constrain the thinker to thinking of the one correct
answer. The instruction to think of a series of digits at
'random' does not preclude the operation of causes
which will result in a series of digits which are anything
but random. The attempt to associate numbers in
'random order' is complicated by the effects of many
unconscious controls. When a mathematician wants to
prepare a truly random series of numbers he has to use
some very sophisticated techniques to obtain what he
wants. So generally when anyone just 'thinks of a
number' his choice may be (unwittingly) the number of
the house in the street in which his girl-friend or his rival
lives. The depth psychologists have given good *prima*

facie evidence that some selection of numbers can be caused by unconscious controls of this kind. So, conversely, when thought is controlled by the instruction to multiply by two mistakes can be made. Such mistakes may be due to 'controls' in the form of bad habits earlier acquired, by odd preference for numbers like 7 or 12 rich in historical or mystical associations, or again by the unconscious controls which the depth psychologists have disclosed. To the psychologist and indeed to every student the explanation of the sources of mistakes can be of greater interest and importance than the explanation of right answers.

3. *That thinking in all its forms is goal-directed, consciously or unconsciously motivated.* All controls or dispositions which give direction to the course of thought have a motivational aspect. This thesis is defended in general terms in the passage quoted from McDougall on p. 14 in which he refers to the manner in which every train of thought is borne along to its end. This thesis, perhaps stated in other words, would command wide acceptance. But less important than the description of general propensities or drives is the more detailed specification of the particular interests, aims, and intentions into which these drives are canalized.

Putting these three theses into a single statement we may say that *all trains of thought are determined (causally) by motivational controls which direct the sequence of ideas to the attainment of some end.* It remains to review some of the chief types of directive controls and to illustrate their influence in some of the common ways of thinking.

Among the simplest types of control are those which psychologists describe as 'sets'. When the subject of an experiment is required to give, say, what number comes to his mind when he is shown the two digits 3 and 5 he is more likely to say 7 or 8 or 15 than he is to say 9 or many other numbers that could be thought of. He is more likely to say 7 if he is 'set' to continuing a sequence (as he might be if he had recently been subjected to an intelligence test of the kind that requires such extrapolation). He would think of 7 as the next odd number. He would be more likely to say 8 if he had recently been occupied with adding numbers, and more likely to say 15 if he had recently been occupied with a task requiring multiplication. This persistence of a set is not just a mechanical process; it is the persistence of a motive, the continuation of a process in which there was something that the Subject was trying to do, the persistence of a *search* for numbers in a sequence, a *search* for sums or products.

Sets of this kind are temporary and evanescent. There are other sets which operate for years and may influence a man's whole style of thought throughout his life. They are habits of thought, and like other habits are formed and sustained by propensities – the abiding interests and sentiments into which propensities are canalized. Some of these are very general and pervasive in their influence, like the scientist's will to be objective or the disposition to ask of every statement: What exactly does this statement mean? What evidence is there for supposing it to be true? Some sets contribute to the success of the search for truth. Others operate in ways which frustrate any such search. A prejudice is a sort of 'set'. It is a predisposition to confirm a preconception, generally derived from what social psychologists describe as 'attitudes', such as 'conservatism' or 'radicalism'. Such attitudes are continuously acting sets, perhaps in some degree constitutional, but certainly the product in part of education, indoctrination, and experience which predisposes a thinker to say 'what is, is pretty good and worth preserving' or to say 'what is, however good it is, could be better. Let us change it.'

Some such sets are represented in consciousness as formulated intentions, principles or policies, aims or purposes of which the thinker is aware. Others are unconscious such as the kinds of 'wishes', the inhibitions, the repressions which the depth psychologists have studied in detail. Some of the many and varied types of directive controls can best be illustrated in a brief review of some of the differing ways of thinking.

'Idle reverie', which at first sight appears to be a simple form of thinking, turns out to be a complex process, but its motivation and its controls become clearer when it assumes the more structured form of the daydream. So with reminiscence. This is never a simple mechanical process like playing back a recording on a tape. It is selective and is a kind of problem solving, a process which has something in common with scientific thinking and often with artistic creation. When a student is asked, for example: 'Tell me, what have you been doing and what has happened to you since we last met?' his report will differ according to whom it is that he is reporting. He will select, reconstruct, and elaborate in different ways. The directing controls will differ according as he is reporting to his parents or to a fellow-student. It will differ again if he is talking to a social group in which he has a reputation as a witty raconteur. He will select, reconstruct, and elaborate in still other ways if he puts his story in the literary form of an autobiography, and it will differ according as he consciously or unconsciously is on the defensive or trying to impress.

There is a quality of memory generally which is described as serviceability. The difference between its presence and absence can be seen by comparing the manner in which a schoolboy may recall a verse of poetry when prompted with the preceding lines with the manner in which a conversationalist or littérateur recalls it to enliven discourse or to illustrate an argument. In the former recollection is tied to a single cue; in the latter it is available for varied applications. This general availability is not dependent upon the variety of the circumstances in which the material was originally presented. The explanation belongs to the psychology of invention. It is a matter of organization of controls.

Novelty in thought is the fruit of a primary and universal function of the mind – a capacity to effect a peculiar mode of synthesis from the raw material with which it is presented. Ultimately there would seem to be two ways in which, in general, novelty may result from synthesis. There is the novelty which issues from the rearrangement of units each of which admits in principle of a separate and independent existence; and there is the novelty which results from the reconstruction of units which can be only abstractly distinguished in a concrete whole but do not enjoy independent being. The first type of synthesis is illustrated by the endless patterns that may be formed from the constituent tiles of a mosaic. The contrasted form is to be seen in the normal process of imagination. When we picture to ourselves a new creation we do not merely re-combine the parts of old and familiar images as we might employ the parts of a jigsaw puzzle; we re-combine the abstract properties of things. Having once seen, say, a yellow square and a blue circle, we can immediately imagine the square to be blue and the circle to be yellow. There is no need to take the two items to bits prior to the re-synthesis. We need not even think of the properties in abstraction. One concrete combination may be followed directly by the other. We perform this elementary operation of re-synthesis even in our dreams.

It was one of the defects of early systems of psychology that this particular mode of re-synthesis received inadequate recognition. The work of imagination was described as though it consisted in the combination and rearrangement of concrete images. But this obviously fails to explain the simplest acts of imaginative thought:

> If 'ifs' and 'ans' were pots and pans
> And all the sea were ink.

We cannot combine anything that we have ever seen of ink, whether bottled or spilt on paper, with any earthly vision of the sea to produce this image. Still less, on such a view, can we deal with the pots and pans.

Properties rather than concrete images are the raw material both of associative processes and of constructive imagination. These synthetic acts, however, do not occur in virtue of any 'mental chemistry', in virtue of any inherent tendencies in ideas spontaneously to combine, though some ideas are inherently suitable for the purpose of constructive thought. The constructive act occurs only as one specific phase in a process directed to an end. It occurs when such a synthesis will provide the solution to a problem; it occurs to satisfy a need.

Some of the most characteristic forms of thinking assume the form of an attempt to solve a problem, and proceed, with some variations, in accordance with the following plan:

(a) A problem is given, or a question raised, together with

(b) Information concerning some of the conditions to which the solution of the problem or the answer to the question must conform. The awareness of the problem and the condition to be satisfied leads on to

(c) The formulation of an hypothesis or the making of a guess regarding possible solutions or answers. The next step is

(d) A process of testing the hypothesis by appropriate activities which may involve observation, recall, association, calculation, deductive, or inductive logical operations, etc. – resulting in

(e) Either a final judgement: 'Yes, that is the answer. It satisfies the test,' or 'No, that won't do. It does not satisfy the conditions.' In the latter case thoughts go back to stage (c) and another hypothesis is formulated or another guess made and the rest of the procedure is repeated. It continues to be repeated until a judgement can be made: 'Yes, that is the answer.'

There are many interesting variants of this plan. Some problem solving processes go on entirely 'in the head' such as performing the tasks set in an intelligence test or a radio quiz. There are other problem solving processes which are almost entirely a matter of observation. In scientific research the processes involve the performance of experiments. In many forms of research in the arts the process is largely a combination of activities which go on in the head with the activity of consulting documents or reference books.

The familiar crossword puzzle can be taken as a very simple paradigm of the sort of problem solving which requires the exercise of a serviceable memory with search through reference books. In this we are required to think of a word in accordance with certain suggestive 'clues'. The clues provide the principal controls. The word, let us say, consists of eight letters. The first of these is S, the fifth is I. It names an English man of letters.

We proceed to guess. 'Sheer guessing' would be completely free association, but the associations are controlled by the clues. All the clues restrict the field of associative exploration. Geographical names do not come to mind, and even the names of persons can be narrowed down to those that begin with S. The possibilities are progressively narrowed down until thought can move in only one direction, and in that direction it can take but a single step. We think of Sheridan. Our problem is solved, and the confirmatory tests are but the work of a moment.

In the case of the crossword puzzle the solution is brought to mind merely by reproduction. The name has been otherwise known. This, however, is not essential. The process is psychologically similar when 'originality' is required – when the novelist, for example, wishes to invent a name.*

In most forms of scientific thought the general plan is not fundamentally different. Here, too, thought commences with a question. The problem is, let us suppose, to ascertain the cause of some obscure disease. Here the question itself increases in complexity concurrently with the advance towards the answer. We may inquire more closely into the symptoms of the disease, study its course, its geographical distribution, the period of life at which it most frequently occurs. The result of such investigation is to augment the number of the facts which any satisfactory answer to our question must explain. It introduces new controls, which stimulate thought in new directions and discourage thought in others.

The facts to be explained constitute what we may call the 'material' controls. They belong, that is to say, to the special subject under investigation. They may be con-

---

* In the notes of Henry James for his unfinished novel *The Ivory Tower* we have preserved to us an interesting document in which this process may be studied. The only important difference in the case of invention is in the nature of the controls.

trasted with the 'formal' controls which are not restricted in their applications to thought in any special branch of science.

It is the function of the 'formal disciplines' to provide the mind with such controls. It was once universally believed that the study of mathematics constitutes such a discipline; but it is now very generally agreed that the value of mathematical training is largely restricted to the control of thought in the investigation of problems to which mathematical considerations are directly relevant. A knowledge of at least elementary statistical techniques has become an essential part of the equipment of the empirical scientist. A case can be made out for the study of Logic as providing universally applicable controls. Familiarity with the general requirements of proof with regard to different kinds of propositions – provided this knowledge has really become embodied in the texture of the mind – may exercise the profoundest influence upon the course of thought. Many problems, for example, admit of being tackled by either an 'inductive' or a 'deductive' method of approach. That is to say, we may attempt to prove a proposition by searching for more general propositions from which it conceivably might be deduced, or we may seek for particular cases which support it. The proclivity to seek deductive proof is perhaps chiefly characteristic of the philosophical cast of mind, whereas the scientific type has a preference for evidence drawn from particular matters of fact. These differences in respect of formal controls are exhibited not only in technical studies; they pervade the whole of common discursive thought. Essayists often exhibit a marked proclivity for a certain logical mould of thought; such as addiction to the use of paradox or the dilemma. There is no reason to suppose that these controlling dispositions belong to an author's inborn constitution.

They are, in general, merely 'habits of mind'. A man acquires skill in the use of the 'dilemma' for aggression or defence as he acquires skill in the use of a rapier for similar purposes.

Sooner or later, provided investigation has been in the right direction – and in this there is always a large element of luck – a final synthesis occurs. Lines of thought converge, the clues cooperate, an 'inspiration' occurs, and the problem is solved. How did this happen?

This final synthetic act has been the object of many a psychological rhapsody and of much misdirected awe. In point of fact, however, an 'inspiration' proves on examination to be a little if anything more than a well-directed guess which happens to be right. Psychologically it differs in no respect from a well-directed guess which happens to be wrong. It is, in any case, one of a series of proposed solutions to the problem. It differs in satisfying all the critical tests. There may be others which satisfy all but one. When, according to the legend, the sight of an apple falling from a tree suggested to Newton the gravitational influence of the earth upon the moon, the guess happened to be right. It failed, however, to satisfy all the relevant clues. It proved to be inconsistent with the existing data regarding the dimensions of the earth. Later it was shown that the critical tests were wrong. Had they not been so we should never have heard of Newton and his apple, though the correction of the data was something with which he had nothing to do.

A well-directed guess becomes an 'inspired revelation' by conforming to the tests. If the tests are altered a discarded theory may be raised to glory. If the rightness of the idea were all-important a man would become a genius very much as he becomes an uncle, through no fault or virtue of his own. But rightness is not the point at all. The virtue lies in the good direction of the guess.

The hall-mark of inventive genius does not lie in the *final* synthesis, but very much further back – in the organization of controls.

Among the clues by which thought is directed and controlled we must distinguish those that are actually productive of ideas from those that are merely critical. The distinction is clearly marked in the crossword puzzle. The clue 'The first letter is S' serves actually to suggest a number of words to mind. Its selective influence operates in preventing the review of irrelevant words. We associate by alliteration. The clue 'The fifth letter is I' operates in an entirely different way. It is not possible to review directly the words which satisfy this condition. The words must be suggested in some other way. The clue supplies a test which can be applied only after a word has come to mind. The distinction between the two kinds of clues does not exclude the occurrence of intermediate cases. Of these we have an example in the clue 'The word consists of eight letters.' We cannot infallibly call to mind words consisting of a specific number of letters, but the clue nevertheless exercises some restriction upon association. It excludes words that are too short and words that are too long. Similar considerations apply to scientific thought. Some facts are definitely suggestive of fruitful lines of reflection and research. Others merely supply the tests to be applied when some solution of the problem has been otherwise conceived.

Thought proceeds mainly under the stimulus of the productive controls. In the crossword puzzle the material is drawn from the reservoir of memory supplemented perhaps by an occasional reference to an encyclopaedia. In scientific research the ratio of reproduction to external investigation is, of course, considerably lower. Even the best-stored mind cannot be in possession of all the relevant facts. Hence the elaborate and highly technical process of research. It is at this point that thought incorporates and directs the process of observation discussed in Chapter 2. It is because observation must be relevant to a problem and, in consequence, be *directed* that we were led to place the primary emphasis upon selection and interrogation.

The application of confirmatory tests, i.e. of the critical controls, is in scientific thought an elaborate affair. The 'guesses' are now 'hypotheses', the implications of which require to be developed before the tests can be applied.* Add to this the complication, previously noted, that with additional knowledge the clues are increasing in number, and the process of thought becomes a highly cooperative affair; extending, perhaps, through many generations. The psychology of thought here requires to be extended into the theory of scientific method.

So much by way of analysis has been required before we could even raise with profit the question: Upon what conditions does the efficiency of thought depend? Under what conditions is a problem solved? How do we get original ideas?

As with other functions, efficiency of thought is partly a matter of motivation, partly one of discipline and control. Strong motivation is essential, since only so are 'difficulties' overcome. The sense of difficulty *is* the consciousness of a problem. The biographers of genius are unanimous in their testimony to the insatiable curiosity of their heroes. The strength of the will to know

* The introduction of 'hypotheses' does not in principle involve anything beyond what we have found in simpler processes of thought. In the crossword puzzle each word suggested is a simple 'hypothesis'. But in this case the tests may be immediately applied. There is no need to develop a chain of implications.

is not merely a matter of the initial intensity of desire but also of its endurance. From the nature of the case the solution of a problem may often require prolonged investigation. Problems of motivation, however, are common to all the functions of the mind, and in consequence are reserved for the final chapter of this book.

Since thought is initiated and sustained by the consciousness of a problem, success will depend upon the manner in which the question is framed, and upon the way in which the question is present to mind. Hence, for example, Descartes' rule of method: 'Method consists entirely in the order and disposition of the objects to which our mental vision must be directed if we would find out any truth. We shall comply with it exactly if we reduce involved and obscure propositions step by step to those that are simpler . . .'* Descartes was here concerned with a somewhat different phase of thought from that with which we are occupied here; but substitute 'question' in place of 'proposition' and we have a generally useful rule.

Perhaps more important than the logical simplicity of the question is the clarity with which it is conceived. In private thought, as well as in public argument, much irrelevance is incurred by vagueness concerning the issue under consideration. *Ceteris paribus*, action is more efficient when we know what we are trying to do and thought is more efficient when we are fully conscious of the question to which an answer is required. This is important precisely because the specific nature of the question provides the dominant controls, the ultimate tests not only of the rightness of the answer but also of the relevance of the hypothesis adduced. It is important, too, to keep as many controls as possible clearly

* Rule V of *Rules for the Direction of the Mind*.

before the mind. This is the intellectual counterpart of 'span of perception'.

Originality, as has been already said, is not the result of striving for novelty as such. Novelty in scientific thought can be, indeed, in a curious way an object of aversion. There is in science as elsewhere a 'resistance to change'. This is one of the 'controls', the 'sets' or dispositions which determine the course of scientific thought. Such resistance can be a form of prejudice, but is not entirely irrational. Scientists try to explain new facts with a minimum of disturbance of existing theory. Freud's revolutionary ideas were for long resisted partly for emotional reasons, but partly because any revolutionary idea is properly accepted only on the basis of carefully tested evidence. The evidence submitted by 'paranormal' psychologists for telepathy has been questioned by reason, partly of emotional prejudice, but also partly (and not unreasonably) because the facts adduced, if established, would upset an enormous corpus of scientific theory not only in psychology but also in well-established biological science and in physics.

Originality is gained in an incidental way in the search for something more important – the solution of some specific problem. Those who are consistently original and inventive are in general those who possess a problem-solving organization of mind. This as a general disposition is, of course, a rare and valuable quality.

There is, however, a democratic equivalent to this aristocratic virtue. This is individuality, and upon this, as a simple pre-condition, creative genius probably depends. Individuality of a legitimate kind may be fostered at every stage of mental life. It is from infancy a common human trait. We all have our idiosyncrasies of physical conformation, of manner and expression. Subject to the elementary conditions of sense and decency, almost any form of individuality has its charm and a certain cultural value. The educational problem is to allow and encourage these individualizing forces to pervade the intellectual life. This need not be left to chance, nor to the caprice of the gods. Individuality depends upon psychological conditions which, in part, we understand and, in part, we can control. It depends in part, upon suitable methods of study, in part, upon the organization of controls. It is a function of the supply of raw material and of the process of manufacture.

Individuality does not work *in vacuo*. Human creation is not creation out of nothing. The biographies of genius report that discovery is the fruit of long and patient study, in the course of which relevant experience is obtained. But more important, perhaps, than the amount of raw material is its composition, and (to continue the economic metaphor) the ratio of material to manufacturing costs. Raw material is required, but material of suitable composition. This is the problem of the dietetics of the mind. A happy combination of studies may be productive of an original synthesis even in the absence of creative genius. Parallel and primarily independent trains of thought will often interact in a generative way. Two ideas will sometimes come together in a novel synthesis with an almost audible click. This is not a matter of their similarities or of their superficial logical relations. Such dynamic interaction often arises (as in the case of verbal wit) from the juxtaposition of incongruous ideas.

In the organization of higher specialized studies there has been perhaps a little over-emphasis of the importance of cognate studies. The continued association of cognate subjects may sometimes, like the marriage of blood relations, lead to sterility. The intermarriage of dissimilars, on the other hand, may exercise a revitalizing effect. This is illustrated by the history of Psychology. For centuries this subject was pursued in intimate connexion with its associated philosophical disciplines. Its progress under these conditions was slow. An impetus was given to development in the nineteenth century by its association with biological studies, and by the introduction into psychology of the technical methods of physics, and of experimental physiology. The application of certain branches of mathematics made possible the development of differentiating mental tests. The introduction of statistical methods into the investigation of memory initiated the studies some of the results of which we have briefly reviewed in Chapter 3. Psychology has had its Copernican revolution without a Copernicus. The change did not depend upon the genius of a single man, but upon the inherent possibilities of interacting ideas. These interactions have occurred in relative independence of the personal qualities of the thinker. Everyone may note similar interactions in the course of daily thought.

The moral to be drawn varies with the stage of study. In elementary education the problem is one of breaking down some of the hard and fast divisions between different scholastic subjects and of stimulating interest in their interrelations. In the private study of the more advanced student what is required is a healthy disregard of the frontiers of his subject. Particularly fruitful is the interchange of 'controls', of allowing historical sense to enter the study of science and of employing scientific methods and scientific concepts in the study of the arts. The happy combination of subjects is, of course, always to be determined on the merits of the case; no rigid principles can be defined.

The second general condition of individuality – perhaps the most important – is to secure the proper distribution of energy between the process of reception and activity of an elaborative type. The disproportionate allocation of time to the former is probably the most serious fault in common methods of study.

The error is not adequately met merely by instructing or exhorting the student 'to think'. This is unpractical advice. There is an important distinction to be drawn between advice which, to be acted upon, merely requires the consent of the recipient's will, and advice which requires to be supplemented by information concerning how it may be carried out. To exhort others to think is like telling them to be clever, or to love their enemies. These injunctions require more than an act of will in order to be obeyed. Many otherwise excellent pieces of advice and many uplifting sermons fail in their purpose through the neglect of this consideration. The mark of the practical counsellor is that he gives advice which can be acted on. It requires merely to be accepted. If the student is to be told to think about his work he must be shown how to do it.

Incidentally he must have something to think about. Thinking is relating. Relating is seeking, and with reasonable luck finding, relations between the things we think about. Some relations are easier to see than others, some are more important than others. The quality of thought is a function of the importance of the relations found. What relations are found will depend chiefly upon what relations are sought. The genius may seek farther afield and make greater discoveries, but in the common search everyone can help. We thus return to the importance of the questioning attitude of mind. What questions may most profitably be raised will vary with the subject; but in any subject there is a limited number of kinds of questions that can be asked. Some of the most common are the following: Why did that happen? What is the connexion between this and that? How is that known? What is the evidence for this assertion? What follows? How is it that so and so is the case when something else is the case; is there no inconsistency? What other examples are there of this sort of thing happening; does it illustrate any general rule? What is the history of this? Is it something quite novel, or has it evolved from something else? From the general analysis we have made of thinking it is obvious that thinking is not all sheer deduction. Deduction is a special case of finding relations of a certain logical type. For those not disposed to deductive reasoning there are other, quite profitable, methods of thought. If the student attends to the nature of the questions raised in the books he reads he will learn the questions to ask appropriate to his subject. Later he will become original by asking questions of his own.

We return then to the maxim: *Let your questions come. Try to get them clear – then follow their lead as far as ever they will go. And, then, ask yourself another question.* Individual and constructive thought, like effective observation and retention, depends upon insatiable curiosity. The awakening of curiosity is the beginning of individuality in the intellectual life. For the question is the most personal and the most individual of our thoughts. Strictly a question cannot be passed from mind to mind. We can communicate only its empty shell. Its inward spirit is a feeling, a kind of pain, the pain we feel when a would-be raconteur gets launched upon an anecdote and then forgets the point.

RESEARCH AND PRODUCTION

Research is often thought of as an esoteric pursuit of high-powered and specially-trained intellectuals. This view is unfortunate. All students are – or at least can and should be – engaged in research. For most students study is a life-long pursuit, whether it takes the form of 'proceeding to research' in a research institution or continuing to take an interest in such things as natural history or local customs, or any of the subjects studied in local societies or in the extra-mural classes provided by universities. (Much good research is carried out by such societies and classes.) This life-long pursuit divides naturally into two phases. The first is that in which the student is just catching up, learning for himself things which are already known by others. The second is that in which he is going beyond what is in the books. Now, the important point is that *psychologically* there is no great difference between the two sorts of study, no great difference between the kind of thinking that goes into research and the kinds of thinking outlined in the first part of this chapter. Research is just search – looking for answers to questions and for solutions to problems. Briefly restated, thinking and research begins with a question – putting into words a specific curiosity. The next step is to make a guess at the answer or to 'formulate an hypothesis'. Psychologically, there is little difference between making a guess and formulating an hypothesis. A botanist wearing his white laboratory overall and surrounded by instruments of precision may formulate the hypothesis that certain chemical substances may facilitate the growth of this or that plant. The same man gardening in his old clothes may get the hunch or make the guess that his broad beans would benefit from an application of this or that fertilizer. The differences between the two situations are matters of comparative detail. They become greater at the next stage, that of testing the hypothesis or hunch. In the laboratory the botanist can control conditions with greater precision. He can use instruments of greater precision to measure effects. Training for botanical research consists in part in acquiring background knowledge, acquiring skill in the use of tools of precision, and skill in the use of the more abstract tools of mathematics, statistics, and the principles of scientific method. But again the differences between the professional botanist and the amateur gardener next door are differences in degree. The amateur gardener can acquire such knowledge and such skills. He may indeed win more prizes at the local show than does the professional botanist.

Methods of finding answers to questions, testing hypotheses and hunches, differ in different fields of research. There are some few kinds of research which can be carried through almost entirely 'in the head'. Philosophy is notoriously an armchair study. Mathematical calculations and the discovery of proofs of a theorem can in principle be done in the head, but in practice they are generally carried out on paper. In some cases the important thing is systematic observation, e.g. recording data about the flora or fauna in a given locality. In many forms of research in the arts the procedure is one of reading relevant books and records, selecting material relevant to the question and the hypothesis entertained. In laboratory research the crucial thing is the performance of experiments. But none of these special activities in itself alone constitutes research or any kind of thinking. Reflection, calculation, deductive reasoning, observation, experiment, etc. are just phases or components of the larger process which consists basically in 'hitting on' a question, 'thinking up' a possible answer, and testing the answer by the appropriate procedures. But even so considered – simply as searching for information or for answers to questions – there is a danger of the idea of research getting out of perspective, as being a much more high-powered activity than it generally is.

The transition from 'finals' to research is less interesting than the transition from 'schooling' to 'productive work' – when 'schooling' means *learning*, in school or college, and 'production' means *doing* something which promotes the health, wealth or happiness of other people in the big world. The distinction, in other words, is that between *intaking* and *outputting*. Research is one form of outputting. Teaching is another form of outputting. So is doing a good job at a petrol pump. All forms of outputting have a certain prestige which intaking often lacks. With prolonged intaking students tend to become impatient. The corrective is to recognize that *productive activity is itself a part of education*. This thesis has been cogently and persuasively presented in a Presidential address to the Institution of Structural Engineers.* The argument is that education has three components: (1) acquiring knowledge from books and lectures (2) acquiring skill in laboratories and workshops (3) gaining self-confidence and other personal qualities through real-life productive activity. What makes this thesis so significant a contribution to the psychology of study and to the philosophy of education is the generality of the principle that productive activity is itself part of the educational process. It is natural that a director of technological education should illustrate the point by referring to the simple case (though not so simple as all that) of the student of the building arts and sciences who is learning to lay bricks. Such a student has to acquire more than a little 'book-knowledge' of the properties of bricks of various kinds, about cementing materials and about many other things. He has to acquire

* Delivered by D. A. G. Reid, Principal of the Brixton School of Building, and published in the Journal of the Institution in December 1965 (Vol. 43, No. 12).

the skills needed for building a wall, straight, level and plumb. To gain these skills he has to build walls *as exercises*, and having built them each is immediately knocked down. But learning through instruction and exercises is not enough. There may be no perceptible difference between the last wall built by the student as an exercise (to be immediately destroyed) and the first wall built on his first job which may stand for a hundred years. But psychologically there is all the difference in the world between building these two walls. The building of the latter is also an *educational* experience. The distinction is universal. The building student's sister may be taking a course of training in cookery classes and the first edible cake she makes she is allowed to take home. His even younger brother may be at an infant school. He, when he completes his first presentable picture does not have it torn up before his eyes. He is encouraged to take it home, and in so doing takes his first modest step as a creative productive artist. The student at the college of building is exceptional. He cannot take his wall home. The principle is not least important in its application to conventional and traditional academic studies. The most characteristic form of production in these studies is *productive writing* – i.e. writing, otherwise than as an exercise, writing something as something not merely for submission to a teacher for critical appraisal. There may be no perceptible difference between the last thing submitted to a teacher for such appraisal and the first thing submitted to a publisher or the editor of a journal, but psychologically there is all the difference in the world.

It is a disturbing thought that our elaborate and expensive educational system turns out so few who have learnt to write – 'write', that is to say, simple, lucid and readable prose of the kind for which publishers and editors clamour. Indeed many, if not most, of those who can 'write' in the required sense have acquired their talent independently of, or perhaps in spite of, their academic studies. The explanation of this is in part that so many traditional methods of teaching students to write are self-defeating and that so many academic exercises *prevent* the student from acquiring the required skill. This comes about in several ways. Examination systems which demand that questions be answered under pressure of time favour slovenly writing. Traditional requirements for the presentation of theses for higher degrees favour the production of research reports which are proverbially unpublishable. One of the basic troubles is that what the student writes – essays, answers to examination questions, theses – is written for submission to a critical teacher or examiner. Hence what he writes tends to be written in an anxious, defensive and cramped style. Good writing is written in a confident, carefree and *individual* style. It is an expression of (to use an overworked word) the writer's '*personality*'. It is directed not so much to real or imagined critics as to those with whom the writer has friendly personal relations. Hence here, more than anywhere else, learning must be in large measure self-directed. What teachers can provide, in addition to helpful criticism, is stimulation and encouragement.

TRAINING FOR RESEARCH AND PRODUCTIVE WRITING

The primary functions of the teacher are not to impart useful information, but to stimulate by every device at his disposal the questioning attitude of mind, and to provide the student with a technical equipment for following up his questions. The requisite technical equipment will vary from subject to subject. It ranges from that involved in the solution of a mathematical problem to that employed in the writing of an essay. At one extreme the problem set admits only of a single answer; at the other it calls for the maximum of individuality. This is, perhaps, the chief limitation of the essay as an instrument of education. It requires the student to fly before he has learnt to walk. Between the extremes of a purely mechanical reproduction of a lesson or the mechanical application of formal rules and the constructive work of an essay many intervening stages require to be traversed.

Of course there is a place for exercises, among the earliest of which is the paraphrase. We have already noted (p. 40) that paraphrasing is an aid to memory, i.e. through encouraging the translation of statements in the 'passive' vocabulary to the 'active' vocabulary. But there is more in paraphrasing than that, much more than meets the eye. It might seem that paraphrasing is a very odd sort of exercise. How, it might be asked, can one paraphrase 'The sky is blue', and why try to? A part of the answer is that to try is to take an opportunity for self-expression – i.e. the expression of one's own personality and so to develop a 'style'. If you write by way of paraphrase 'Blue is the sky!' you indicate that for you the blueness of the sky is a rather romantic fact. If you write 'The sky is *blue, blue, blue!*' you show how worked up you are about the blueness of the sky. If you open your first novel with the words 'The sky was blue, a hard icy blue as Robin walked behind his mother's coffin to her grave', you give due warning to the reader that worse is to come in the story of Robin's life. If you write 'The light from the sky is B24 on the standard colour chart' or that it is of such-and-such a wave-length, you indicate how very scientific you wish to be.

In more complicated cases a good objective in writing a paraphrase is to try to improve on the statement paraphrased. It is often possible for a student to restate a difficult passage from a textbook with greater clarity than the original. This, indeed, is another important function of a teacher. He paraphrases differently according to whom his lesson or lecture is addressed. He restates the theory of evolution or the principle of relativity differently according to whether he is talking to twelve-year-olds, to sixth-formers, to university students or to the general reading public. Another exercise allied to the paraphrase is that of translating experience into words. A student should try to acquire the ability to give a plain, descriptive report of a simple sequence of events – an account, say, of an accident in the street. This should possess the elementary merits of simplicity, accuracy, and coherence which would commend it to the police. Next he should be able to reproduce, 'in his own words' and in a simplified and condensed form the substance of a reasoned argument. The essential requirements here are brevity, precision, and a sense of logical connexion. The next stage is the commentary. The student should acquire facility in the expression of his personal 'reaction' to a passage read. The comment may be one of elucidation, illustration, logical, factual, or literary criticism. The sole essential condition to which judicious comment must conform is that it should fall within the generous bounds allowed by *relevance*. Technical exercises appropriate to special branches of study, so far as they are not mechanical, are variations and elaborations of the comment. The full-dress essay is the last and most difficult member of the series. It requires the most complex organization of individual controls.

TRAINING FOR RESEARCH AND
PRODUCTION

Research begins in the nursery. No one can be more research-minded than a two-year-old child exploring the odd world in which he finds himself. What education and training can do is first to keep alive this curiosity, the appetite of the mind, and second to canalize this curiosity into appropriate channels. Training also provides the tools of research and develops skill in the use of these tools. It leads the young research student to the growing point of knowledge. Not least important is the training it can give in the arts of communication, in writing research reports. To keep alive and canalize curiosity is the chief of the teacher's responsibilities. It is also the teacher's responsibility to expedite the passage to the growing points of knowledge. These growing points can be reached very early. So much so that serious research can begin in the secondary school.* Such training in the techniques of research and the use of the tools of research continues in the universities and other institutions of post-secondary education. But throughout, skill in reporting lags behind skill in doing. The two-year-old researcher exploring his world cannot report his discoveries. At school and at the university, students learn the technical language of their science, which facilitates communication with fellow scientists but forms a barrier to communication with others. This barrier can progressively mount as the student progresses through

* In 1957 a committee was set up by the Council of the Royal Society to provide and guide scientific research in schools. By 1961 research projects were in operation in sixty-eight British schools. A brief account of this very important development can be found in *The Advancement of Science*, Vol. XVIII, No. 74, November 1961.

undergraduate to post-graduate research. It is not just a matter of giving formal instruction in the use of the English language. It is less a matter of instruction than a kind of therapy; it is a matter of treating certain inhibitions and emotional attitudes which interfere with communication. Indeed, it is perhaps more a matter of preventive treatment, and it is never too early for the student to begin to train himself in the writing of reports. If research begins in the nursery, training in the writing of research reports can begin not later than with the young student's first essay – say 'On a Day in the Country'. There are no sharp lines of transition from writing this first essay to writing a thesis for the Ph.D. degree. From writing his first essay the schoolboy goes to write another on, say, 'An Excursion of the School Natural History Society'. In his secondary school he is encouraged to write up part of the research report on some collective study of the kind (referred to above) which is being supported by the Royal Society say on 'A comparison of protozoan life in the upper and lower reaches of the Thames'. As an undergraduate he will be encouraged to design, carry out, and report on some small experimental project or field study. He will then be ready to 'proceed' to postgraduate research say on 'Physical properties of beryllium'.

With research reports at the postgraduate level there will be cases that will be found to differ in their requirements – the thesis presented for a higher degree, and what may be called for short 'a report to management' – that is, the sort of report submitted by a member of a research staff in an industrial organization. At each stage of his research the student will receive guidance from a teacher, a tutor, or a director of research. But there are limits to what the tutor can do. The acquisition of skill in reporting is perhaps the clearest example of the principle that study is self-directed. The tutor can say: 'Look! This passage in your report is frightfully obscure. I think you should rewrite it.' What he cannot do or what he should not do, is to say how in detail it should be rewritten. This would be to write the thesis or report himself. Nor can the student get the needed instruction merely by reading further books or attending further lectures. There are, however, a few general guiding ideas which may help the student to teach himself how to write a thesis or research report.

1. The importance of deciding in advance to whom the report is addressed.

Before putting pen to paper the writer of an essay, a thesis or report should ask himself: For whom is this piece of writing to be written? Writing is a social art, a form of communication. Writing to oneself is as eccentric as talking to oneself. Writing into the blue is as eccentric as talking into the blue. Accordingly the Golden Rule is: Always, *always* pin up a picture in your mind's eye of the person or persons to whom or 'at' whom your communication is directed, and all the time keep this picture vivid and clear.

The rule applies to the first essay on 'A Day in the Country'. Its content, its form and its style will vary according as it is written for Teacher to mark and 'correct' or written as a letter home to intelligent, sympathetic, and interested parents. The principle applies to the essay or 'paper' written at the university. The content, form, and style will vary according as it is written 'for' a tutor to read or written to a fellow-student, some friendly critic or critical friend. Not less important than papers written for a tutor during the university term are letters written to fellow-students during the vacation. It is a good thing for a student to write to a fellow-student about some bright idea he has thought up, or attacking some favourite theory which his friend has espoused. A writer's characteristic and individual style develops more through such informal correspondence than in writings directed to unknown and unpictured readers.

Some writings are directed to more than one kind of reader. Some theses are written simply with the examiners in mind. Other theses, and these are generally better theses, are written having not only the examiners in mind but also the readers of a learned journal in which the research might be published or readers in some larger public, the members of which are well placed to turn the results of research to some useful account. Those who write theses for higher degrees could be encouraged more than they usually are to regard their examiners as transparent, to look through them to other readers. They would then write so that the main contents of the thesis would be in a form suitable for publication and they would put into appendices statistical and other technical details necessary for satisfying the examiners that the conclusions drawn are sufficiently supported by the evidence adduced.

Similar considerations apply to research reports addressed to Management. What 'Management' wants is chiefly a *clear* statement of the problem studied, and a *clear* statement of the conclusions reached and some concrete suggestions regarding the implementation of the conclusions. Technical details, and the evidence that the conclusions and suggestions are well founded in the light of the evidence adduced will be referred by Management to Management's other specialist and technical advisers.

2. *The importance of being bilingual in reporting on research.*

It follows, inescapably, from the foregoing considerations that those who report on research must be bilingual in the sense that they must be able to talk and write the language appropriate for communication with examiners, fellow experts, and other technical and specialist referees, but also be able to talk and write the language appropriate for communication with a larger public of educated intelligent readers who without specialist knowledge are in a position to implement the findings of research. Accordingly most research reports need to be written in two forms – one for each class of reader. Training for technical reporting is in the main taken care of in the school and in the university or other institutions of post-secondary education and research. The acquisition of skill in translating the substance of technical reports into a form suitable for the non-specialist is primarily the responsibility of the research student himself.

3. *The importance of feedback.*

Acquiring skill in reporting in all its forms, like acquiring any skill, depends upon the principle of 'feedback'. One of the best established and practically important results of the scientific study of learning is that the Subject must be kept informed of the results of his attempt to make the right response. This depends on the feedback of information regarding the success of the attempt. The same principle applies in teaching. The teacher learns to teach and improve his teaching by receiving back information as to his success or failure in getting the lesson across. It is for this reason that examinations can be a test of the teacher as well as of the student. The value of feedback varies with the speed and frequency with which the information is returned. The research worker reporting on research has a function similar to that of the teacher. He is in fact teaching others what he has learnt himself. Like the teacher his success depends upon the speed with which the relevant knowledge of success or failure is returned. This is the basic reason why before submitting the report to the ultimate arbiter the research worker should try out the report upon a fellow research worker – or a representative of the kind of reader for whom the report is intended.

CHAPTER 5

On Motivation and the Will to Work

What questions has this Will to truth not laid before us!
— Nietzsche (*Beyond Good and Evil*)

THE older textbooks of Psychology devoted many pages to 'The Will'. Modern texts rarely mention the word. The older texts were largely concerned with such philosophical questions as that of the 'freedom of the will' and such questions as: Can we will ourselves to do something which we know to be impossible? These are interesting questions but questions which do not lend themselves to investigation by the methods of empirical research. 'The Will', as a certain kind of faculty or power, is not nowadays seriously considered. There are indeed questions about self-control, motivation in work, which can be profitably studied, and which are studied, for example, in terms of Freud's concept of the Super-Ego and in terms of the incentives which influence the performance of a worker at the bench. There are also questions about self-control of importance in daily life and questions of special interest to the student, how to concentrate, how to deal with all the enticements which distract him from his books – simple practical questions to which provisional answers can be given. If there is no such thing as 'The Will' there may be forces included by expressions like Nietzsche's 'Will to truth', or the 'will to learn', the 'will to work'.

The ultimate source of efficiency in observation, in memory, and in constructive thought is insatiable curiosity and the itch to know. How is this itch produced?

As often as not it is a simple infection, caught from a

teacher or friend. There have been many scientific inquiries into how we come to like the things we do like and into how students get interested in one subject rather than another. Some facts are fairly well established, e.g., that likings for subjects of study are often derived from likings for people who teach these subjects. More surprising, perhaps, is the fact that human beings can come to like almost anything. Students can get interested in almost any subject. Some people have acquired a taste for eating tallow candles. Many students have become interested in the irregular verbs of dead languages. Of course it is understandable that people like doing the things they can do well. On the other hand, some people undervalue the things they can do easily and aspire to talents which they do not and never could possess. The fact is that 'Human nature is a rum 'un' and there remains much to be explained.

There can be no doubt that students should be encouraged to do as well as they can the things they can do best. To say this however might seem to run counter to a venerable principle of educational discipline, viz. that for the development of 'character' students should make themselves do, or be made to do, things they do not like doing. William James, in his charming and persuasive way, advised us to 'keep the faculty of effort alive by a little gratuitous exercise every day' – to do something every day for no other reason than the fact we do not want to do it. It was James the moralist rather than James the psychologist who said this. The venerable doctrine of discipline is a misinterpretation of an important truth. The truth is that we keep the 'faculty of effort alive' by doing something *difficult* – which can be a good reason for liking to do it. However, for everyone there is an appropriate level of difficulty. This is true both for work and play. Games like ludo or noughts and crosses are too easy for many and they pall. Chess, on the other hand, is for many too difficult to play very well. For everyone there is an optimal level of difficulty and an optimal 'level of aspiration'. The rough rule is: try to do things at which you have a 50-50 (or perhaps one in three) chance of success.

Today, psychologists are inclined to say: Don't try to make yourself do anything you do not want to do. Try, rather, to make yourself want to do it when you believe that it is a good thing to want. But this too is a dark saying needing elucidation and qualification. The fact is that we cannot *make* ourselves want anything whatever – at least not directly and not by sheer willing. We cannot *make* ourselves love our neighbours when in fact they are really objectionable neighbours. What we can do is to expose ourselves to the forces which tend to make us more tolerant. And so it is with getting to like things we do not like, and with getting interested in studies which we have found boring. We can expose ourselves to the forces which induce tolerance and, after that, liking. What are these forces?

They do not include 'sheer will power' or a 'faculty of concentration'. The 'will' and 'the power of concentration' are among the unhelpful abstractions which are outmoded in contemporary psychology. But these concepts are not just discarded. They are replaced by other concepts in a different approach. 'John', his teacher reports, 'is bone lazy and does not concentrate.' The truth may be that John is very energetic and is concentrating on things in which his teacher lacks interest. John is thinking about the new fishing-rod that has been promised to him for his birthday. What his teacher is reporting is *his own* inability to distract John's attention from fishing-rods to the procedures for extracting square roots.

The successful teachers who know how to distract John's attention from fishing rods to square roots have by intuition, experience, and good common sense anticipated in some degree the discoveries of the psychologists who have invented scientific methods for *manipulating* the human will. 'Manipulation' is an unpleasant word, but it draws our attention to the fact that the will is not like a muscle which can be strengthened by effort, or by 'a little gratuitous exercise every day'. It is rather that men are led to behave sensibly and to do the right thing by a great variety of stimulations and inducements, and by the organization of circumstances. These manipulations or techniques of control have been developed by industrial psychologists and practitioners of the new science of Ergonomics (the science of work) and by experts in what is called 'motivational research'.

It is now sufficiently established that for any conventional working period, such as a day or a week, there is a characteristic 'work curve' – a graph which sets out the fluctuations in working efficiency for that period. For example, a working day with morning and afternoon periods will often show a curve like this: It begins at a level below the best and there is a progressive improvement to a point of greatest efficiency followed often by a decline towards the break for the midday meal. In the afternoon there is often a similar sequence – a period of warming up, a period of high efficiency, and a terminal decline at the end of the working day. There are, of course, variations in different kinds of work and variations in accordance with the different incentives which are operating; but there are some broad explanatory principles which apply to many forms of work, including the work of the student.

The will to work, whether that of the operative at the factory bench or that of the student at his desk, is variable in a number of respects, each of which is in considerable measure controllable and *self-controllable*.

Whenever there is an *intention* to do something we can distinguish (i) its *objective* (*what* we intend to do), (ii) its *intensity* (*how much* we want to do it), (iii) its *duration* (for *how long* we want to do it), (iv) the *time* or *times* of occurrence (*when* we want to do it) and (v) a character which, for want of a better word, we can describe as its '*polarity*' (its appetitive or aversive nature).

The circumstances which influence each of these variable features of an intention determine the effectiveness of that intention.

(i) *Objectives*. Whenever we want to do something there is something that we want to do. This is the objective or goal of our intention. There is, of course, no end to the list of things that people can want. There are innumerable specific wants and many non-specific wants. We can distinguish in hunger, for example, quite specific cravings from non-specific appetites. Pregnant women and convalescents often have very specific cravings. 'It must be fillet steak and nothing else will do.' Contrasted with this is non-specific hunger: 'Give me something to eat. I don't mind what. I am just ravenous.' So with our curiosities. 'How's Uncle Bob? Is his arthritis better?' is to be contrasted with 'Well, what's the news?' In general, study directed by specific questions is more effective than non-specific curiosity, but it must be added that there is some evidence that great intellectual success is often associated with the breadth of a student's curiosities.

Under 'objectives' must be included the targets and standards which reflect 'levels of aspiration'. A person who is practising a skill may say to himself 'Today I am going to do my best, I am going to get the highest score I can'. Or he may say 'Last time I scored 60 per cent, today I am going to aim at 70 per cent'. There is experimental evidence that the latter kind of intention (specific) is more effective than the vaguer or less specific intention of 'doing one's best'. There is also evidence that for every kind of practice there is an optimal level of aspiration. Some people think they should always aim at 'perfection' or other very remote objectives. Others lack self-confidence. They do not aim high enough. In practising a high jump an athlete who has cleared five feet may say 'Now I will go for *six* feet'. Another may say 'Now I must go for five feet one'. The former is an unrealistic level of aspiration, the latter insufficiently ambitious. So far as a general rule can be given, it is that a higher level of aspiration is appropriate for the early stages, but that the sights must be progressively lowered. This is because learning in general is most rapid in the early stages and becomes slower as the ultimate limits of ability are reached.

In short, targets or objectives should be '*personal, proximate* and *precise*'. This is a slogan or mnemonic phrase to remind us (i) that targets should be set with due regard to realistic estimates of our own personal capacity (the 50-50 chance of success), (ii) that we should go first of all for the next stage, not first of all for the ultimate perfection, and (iii) that we should define the immediate objective as precisely as we can – say to 10 per cent or to 5 per cent improvement on present performance.

(ii) *The intensity of desires.* Social reformers, preachers, propagandists and others whose calling is to inspire us have frequently conceived their mission as one of intensifying the desire to do what is good. In this the emphasis has been misplaced. Intense desires which are reinforced by strong emotions are most appropriate for *emergency situations*. If you are being chased by a bull, or if your house is on fire, there is a need to get a move on if you feel strongly about the situation. But the strength of a desire is not just a matter of emotional intensity. Intense desires can be very transitory. In fact they generally must be. In acting under an intense desire we are so to speak living on our capital, our reserve of energy, and this has to be repaid later by emotional fatigue or the sort of reaction which is so often experienced by those who take part in 'revivalist' meetings. Perhaps most serious is the fact that intense desires tend to express themselves in 'regression' and primitive behaviour. Intensely motivated reformers are revolutionists, however good their causes, are apt to indulge in senseless destruction and sheer cruelty. Even in ordinary life righteous indignation can lead quite nice people to do or say things which they will soon regret. Skilled activities are best carried out with cool deliberation. A good boxer does not lose his temper. A good billiards player or a good golfer never strikes out wildly. The strength of a desire is less a matter of its 'intensity' than it is a matter of its duration (persistence) and its other temporal features. Cool, steady purposes, which psychologists describe as 'interests' or 'sentiments', can be 'stronger' forces than emotions.

(iii) *The duration of desires.* Most desires are periodic. They arise at certain times, last for a certain time and then wane, commonly to arise again later. In speaking of concentration the emphasis is upon duration, the time for which an interest, or some form of curiosity, dominates consciousness and behaviour. We can contrast the fleeting interest aroused by a conundrum or puzzle which provokes the response – 'Give it up. What's the answer?' with the sort of interest which provokes the response 'No, don't tell me; I will find the answer myself.' In the latter case the student may work to midnight and beyond in his effort to solve the problem. This sort of difference is to be seen also in the behaviour of very young children. Psychologists have found new names for the old-fashioned concept of perseverance – 'perseveration' or 'obsessional behaviour', but we still await complete explanations of perseverance, perseveration and obsessional behaviour. In the meantime we may continue to respect such behaviour as one of the criteria of a student's calibre as a scholar.

(iv) *The times of occurrence of desires*. Much depends on *when* a desire occurs or a decision is made. The good intentions with which Hell is said to be paved are perhaps, in the main, intentions which occurred *at the wrong time*. It is all very well to say, when at the end of term the marks of an exam are put up, 'Oh, how dreadful! I must work harder "next term".' But the vacation intervenes during which another paving stone has gone to Hell. So, too, a worker on piece rates may be disappointed by his Friday pay packet. 'Golly', he says, 'I must get a move on next week.' But even a short week-end is long enough for yet another paving stone to go to Hell. It is a pity that examination marks cannot be announced at the beginning of a term and pay packets distributed on Monday mornings. The principle is that *good intentions are more effective when conceived at the time when they can be given immediate expression*.

Those clever manipulators of the will, the advertisers and salesmen of encyclopedias know a lot about all this. At one time they used to send attractive advertisements with the suggestion that we order now, sending a small deposit, etc. To which we reacted by saying to ourselves 'How marvellous! Yes I must have that, but I haven't time to write now. Besides I must buy a postal order for the deposit'. But before we ever got to the post office another paving stone had gone to Hell. The salesman now knows this. Today we receive the alluring description of the encyclopedia together with a stamped addressed envelope. In this in accordance with instructions 'Put a cross in the space marked *Yes Please but pay nothing now – you can pay later in easy instalments. Post this card today.*' Everything has been thought of. There is nothing to frustrate the impulsive will to buy, which is also an impulsive will to know all that an encyclopedia can teach us. Every facility is provided to enable an intention to find expression at the very moment at which the impulse is experienced.

(v) *'Polarity'*. This semi-technical term comes from the contrast between the two ends of a magnet – at one pole it attracts and at the other it repels. So with desires, there are attractions and repulsions. Desires are sometimes described as positive or negative. Most desires, like magnets, are *both* positive and negative: they contain both attractions and repulsions, they contain both an attraction to one thing and an aversion from something else. The normal appetite for food contains both an attraction to some edible thing, and an aversion from the pangs of hunger. So, too, studious curiosity contains attraction towards certain kinds of knowledge and aversion from the ignominy of ignorance. Motivation is often described in terms of 'rewards' and 'punishments'. The student is rewarded not only by prizes and approbation. He is also rewarded by the satisfaction inherent in the success in gaining knowledge and solving problems. He is punished not only by formal penalties but also by disappointment, and by the punishment inherent in any kind of failure of achievement. There has been much discussion of the relative value of reward and punishment in learning. There is some scientific evidence that 'rewards' are more effective than 'punishments', but there is no conclusive evidence against the common-sense judgement that the combination of suitable rewards and suitable punishments is more effective than either rewards or punishment alone. (The qualifications implied by 'suitable' are important.)

In the light of this breakdown of the 'will to work' into what are in principle measurable and controllable components we can take a new look at the 'work curve' of the student engaged in study. This curve is clearly the result of many forces. The chief of these forces or factors are those that influence variations in *ability* and those that influence variations in *inclinations*. The major spells of work are usually in mid-periods of relatively high efficiency preceded by and followed by periods of lower levels of efficiency. The earliest period is the warming up phase in which initial inertia has to be overcome. The third phase in which there is a decline of efficiency is commonly to be attributed to 'fatigue'. Everyone has experienced 'initial inertia' and 'fatigue', but neither has been completely explained. Fatigue has been described as loss of capacity due to previous work. Initial inertia might be described as loss of capacity due to previous relaxation from work. But neither are simply loss of *capacity*. Both involve loss of *incentive* or the loss of the *inclination* to work. In both we can distinguish 'objective' and 'subjective' aspects. Objective fatigue is shown in observable and measurable declines in speed and accuracy of work. Subjective fatigue is shown in the private, introspectable but reportable feelings of the worker in bodily sensations, aches and pains, the experience of boredom, in sleepiness and the felt disinclination to work. Similar distinctions can be drawn between objective and subjective manifestations of initial inertia.

One of the best established facts concerning fatigue

(and this applies too to initial inertia) is that there is no simple relation between the objective and the subjective manifestations. There can be pronounced feelings of fatigue without signs of objective fatigue and vice versa. This should not be surprising if there is anything in the plausible suggestion that the feelings of fatigue are not so much indications of present objective fatigue as warning signals of impending objective fatigue. On this view the mechanism of subjective fatigue is a safety device provided by nature to *prevent* objective fatigue. It works like one of those petrol gauges which record zero when there is still a gallon or so in the tank.

However that may be, the subjective signs of fatigue should be taken seriously. They at least indicate an impending need for rest or relaxation. In normal work there should be regular steady spells of activity at a reasonable level of effort separated by equally regular spells of rest and recreation. A rough general rule for the avoidance of undue fatigue may be stated in the following terms. Some form of relaxation should be taken for a few consecutive minutes in every hour; work should cease for two or three consecutive hours in every day; one complete day of rest and recreation should be reserved in every week; and a holiday of from two to three consecutive weeks should be taken after several months of work.

The case is different with the phase of initial inertia. Felt disinclinations to start work can be dealt with more ruthlessly. Here if anywhere, is the case for the exercise of 'will power', but will power can be supplemented by innocent devices of self-manipulation. A useful instrument for the control of felt disinclination is the time-table. To operate a time-table is a laudable way of working to rule. Responsibility is transferred from the will and put in the charge of the clock. Probably the majority of distinguished students have been creatures of habit. Housewives, it is said, could tell the time of the day by observing the movements of Immanuel Kant. But the time-table should be used with intelligence and discretion. It is an instrument for starting us on our course and should not be used primarily as a brake. Much is gained if we can plan our daily round and reduce it to routine. Attention should be paid more especially to the signals at the beginning and at the end of the major periods of study. Internal subdivisions are the better for being elastic, and they may be quite ruthlessly ignored when occasion demands. The length of the working period naturally will vary with the nature of the work. Periods of mechanical memorization should, as we have seen, be short. So should periods of work which require maximum concentration. Periods devoted to reflective reading, and to the performance of practical exercises, can of course be considerably longer. In general, it is better to devote two or three consecutive hours to a single subject than to attempt to reproduce in private study the routine of the school. These longer periods may be diversified by changes in the method of work. For example, we can alternate written work with reading. Short intervals of rest, five to ten minutes in duration, may with advantage be introduced each hour. On the same general principle it repays the student to form reasonably regular habits in the matter of times for taking meals, of rising and of going to bed. All this of course is a matter of common sense rather than of meticulous organization.

On the vexed question of the midnight oil we must avoid fanaticism. On the whole, the consensus of experienced opinion is that morning work is the most efficient. This belief is reinforced by physiological and psychological evidence. The great thing is to avoid squandering the valuable morning hours. Night-work, however, may claim keen supporters, and there are some weighty considerations on their side. Provided that the day has not been exhausting, night-work benefits from the cumulative suggestions of the day: the seeds which have been sown in the course of reading or at lectures begin to germinate; and at night thought flows easily. Moreover, some of the distracting influences of the day have become less potent. Distractions may have their origin in the body as well as in external causes. Lack of exercise may itself be distracting. The healthy body, like a horse fed on oats, requires self-expression. Fidgety behaviour and a sense of restlessness are sometimes symptomatic of the thwarted need for physical action. When these insistent demands are satisfied the body, so to speak, curls up and goes to sleep, leaving the mind in sole possession of the field. Provided, therefore, that exercise has not been exhausting, slight bodily fatigue may be beneficial. For such reasons night study of an appropriate nature may be very profitable, and in most cases the work performed at night will be superior to that of the afternoon.

Intrusive trains of thought are not effectively disposed of merely by repression. They must either be inhibited at their source or allowed a measure of satisfaction. To attempt to arrest them in full flight, when they have reached their full acceleration, is wasteful of energy. A wandering thought is often symptomatic of an un-completed purpose. The neglect to answer a letter may be the cause of much distraction. The rankling of an insult to which we failed on the spur of the moment to find an apt retort may spoil a morning's work. We have noticed, too, the insistence of the body in its call for exercise. In many such cases it pays us well to make a little concession to the weakness of the flesh – to give it rein a while. We may write the neglected letter, or purge ourselves of passion by a walk, and a little concentrated thought upon the matter that disturbs us. Under such conditions the thwarted impulse may be more quickly put to rest.

It is better, whenever possible, to stem the current of distraction at its source. The difficulty of settling down to work and of maintaining concentrated attention may arise from the interest of a previous conversation, from an unfinished novel, or from a chess problem which we have left unsolved. Such sources of distraction may sometimes be circumvented by a change in the organization of leisure. One reason why certain forms of sport provide the best use of leisure time is that the game is self-contained: it leaves so few untidy ends. Conversation, on the other hand, always throws out runners, and the better the conversation the farther the runners go.

A time-table, fairly firm but also flexible, is of special importance in vacation study. In school or college terms the time-table is imposed for administrative convenience. In vacations it is a matter for self-directed study. It is a useful way of dealing with initial inertia and for circumventing distractions – both internal and external.

The most serious of internal distractions is worry. It can be the first sign of a nervous breakdown, and suicide among students is more frequent than it should be. But to entertain thoughts of suicide is *quite* inexcusable. No examination in the world is all that important. It is better to say 'To hell with my career in medicine (or what not), I will chuck it all up and take a job at a petrol pump.' This is better. After all there have been men who started at a petrol pump and ended in the House of Lords. This is a more sensible reaction, but also a bit melodramatic. Besides it is *premature*. There is an ineradicable element of luck, good and bad, in all examinations. Quite a few students who are prepared for failure get through at a commendable level. Wait until the examination results are published. If the worst happens that is quite soon enough to think about the petrol pump.

In the meantime reflect as coolly and rationally as you can along the following lines: Think first of all that the worst happens in this world about as often as the very best happens – neither of which happens very often. What happens most often is something between the two. But start with the worst of all possible outcomes. What to do then? Face up to that, still keeping cool and rational. Well, there will still be a job at the petrol pump. Then go on from that to the next worst thing that could happen and to the next worst after that. Sooner or later, if you still keep cool you will come to the thing that will most probably happen.

Then you go on to reflect along the following lines. *The antidote to worry is action* – always, always action, and if possible *action now*. The Devil may then whisper in your ear. 'But there is nothing you can do. The situation is hopeless'. Well, if nothing can be done there is nothing to do, so why worry? But there is very rarely a situation in which literally nothing can be done. Suppose you lie awake one night, worrying, tossing about, turning from side to side, not being able to think what to do. Worry at night is particularly troublesome because at night there is so little one can do. But there is one thing you can do. Get out of bed and make yourself a cup of tea. While you are drinking your tea write a letter. It can be to *The Times*, or to a teacher or to a sympathetic friend. In this letter let yourself go, let out everything that is on your mind – and in the strongest terms. You will feel a little better after that. Do not go out and post this letter. The last post has been collected. Besides, in the morning you may wish to revise it. Go back to bed.

Akin to worry is the state of anxiety. In some ways anxiety is worse since it is apt to last longer, but the first-aid remedy is the same as for worry. Do something, preferably something you know you can do rather well, something that helps you to regain self-confidence. Study and the pursuit of knowledge is generally pleasurable. The efficient exercise of any function is normally pleasurable. If the practice of study is painful, something is almost certainly wrong – an unfortunate choice of subjects, defective methods of work, or faulty working conditions. The best results are never secured by feverish energy born of the fear of failure. Most commonly, perhaps, the student is worried by the 'difficulty' of his subject; but difficulties looked at the right way up may be a source of pleasure. The sense of difficulty is by no means always to be attributed to personal limitations. In fact, if our findings in Chapter 4 are substantially correct, all our studies should be 'difficult', full of problems; and the process of solving them would be the normal source of pleasure in intellectual pursuits. Perhaps the reason why students do not more frequently take their pleasures in this way is partly because they are apt to be harassed by an overcrowded syllabus which leaves no time for thought, and partly because the sense of difficulty has come through faulty educational methods to be associated with a sense of subjective limitation. There are, however, intrinsically difficult subjects – subjects essentially consisting of a set of problems. These never can and never should be easy. They are inherently difficult, not only to the student but also to the teacher. If the novice thinks he understands a work on the first casual reading this in itself is sufficient proof that he hasn't. He is only beginning to understand it when he finds it difficult. This applies to some parts of most subjects. It is a misunderstanding of the situation when difficulty of this kind is introjected as a sense of personal incompetence. The trouble is aggravated by the application of inappropriate standards of progress and by the pursuit of inappropriate ideals. Commonly, the student expects to progress at the same rate in these subjects as in easy subjects, and failing to do so blames himself or complains of the limitation of his powers. But there is a fundamental difference between progress in 'easy' and progress in 'difficult' subjects. The characteristic of an 'easy' subject is that its facts, individually, are not difficult of comprehension. The only problem is to assimilate, organize, and apply. Under such conditions progress may be perceptibly rapid, and this engenders confidence. In the 'difficult' subject (and the difficult parts of an easy subject) the facts themselves, through their abstractness or their complexity, require an effort of thought merely to be understood. The process of mere assimilation is slow and gradual. The student, obsessed by the ideal of erudition, is discouraged by his apparent lack of progress, even where progress may be all the greater by reason of being slow. In such subjects haste results in vagueness, superficiality, and increasing confusion of thought, where the appropriate ideals are accuracy and clarity of mind. A difficulty should always be dealt with in a cool and deliberate way, and with an oriental disregard of time. Effort spent on difficulties should also be well distributed. The intervals of quiet consolidation are as important as the periods of concentrated thought. These considerations apply even when the difficulty does in fact arise from individual limitations. Lack of self-assurance is perhaps the most serious emotional disability in the intellectual life, and its roots run deep. It is perhaps almost universal. The student only slowly and imperceptibly emerges from a state in which self-depreciation is most amply justified. From birth the child is accustomed to dependence. He is more ignorant than his elders, and his independent judgements are almost certain to be wrong. He is accustomed to being told what he should believe, and to the arbitration of authority. What 'it says' in the book tends to be taken as final. That the book was written by some human and fallible hand is a late and devastating revelation. Apart from the special stimulus of encouragement, the measure of independence appropriate to intellectual maturity is liable to be delayed. Ultimately, self-confidence requires a rational foundation. Non-rational suggestions may be useful in countering equally non-rational causes of diffidence; but in the last resort it is desirable that we should face our tasks with confidence based upon a dispassionate appreciation of attested merits. It is something gained if we at least escape the domination of inhibiting ideas. There has been a tendency in recent years to underestimate the influence of mere ideas upon the emotional life. It is true that we cannot awaken idealism merely by preaching abstract principles. Nevertheless there are some ideas which are naturally congruent with enthusiasm, and there are some that stultify. The remedy is to make the most of the powers with which we are endowed, to find rational grounds for self-confidence by doing as well as we can what we can do best. Moreover, we might be a little more exacting in our demand for proof of our own incompetence. Incidentally it may be noted that the proof of the absence of ability is always rather longer than the proof that it is present. If we have *once* performed a task, that is sufficient proof that we can do it. A single failure, on the other hand, is not sufficient proof that we cannot.

Trite though it be to say so, success may depend upon repeated effort. It may depend too upon the time at which we try. It may be suspected that the prevalence of the 'mathematic phobia' is due to the fact that certain branches of mathematics which can be acquired later are often taught several years before the required powers of abstraction have matured.

Lack of self-assurance may also be due to certain special illusions. One that is very common almost deserves a special name. It might be called the fallacy of 'the misplaced average'. The normal man possessed, let us say, of normal powers of retention tends to believe that his capacity to remember is below the average. This is due, perhaps, to the fact that he is more frequently confronted with the cases of his own failure to remember than with those of other men. When they recall what he cannot, he is aware both of their success and of his own failure. When, on the other hand, he remembers where others have forgotten, there is often nothing to show that his own performance is superior. Whatever the explanation, such illusions are of common occurrence.

In the cultivation of rational self-confidence much depends upon the teacher. That teachers do not do more in this respect is perhaps due to the fear that the deliberate stimulation of self-confidence will merely engender self-conceit. The danger, however, is not very great. More students suffer from a deficiency of confidence rather than from an excess. It is not a good thing to be very preoccupied with the assessment of one's own abilities, but it is quite a good thing to try to assess one's own abilities in a cool, objective way – avoiding excessive modesty as well as excessive conceit. As both the worst and the best rarely happen it is not easy to be either at the top or at the bottom of the class. Most of us fail to attain either form of distinction but find ourselves somewhere in between.

This chapter has grown into something like a sermon, and a long sermon at that. We can bring it to an end in a rather selective summary:

The 'problem of concentration' is a problem of the will to work. Now, there are three ways in which we may attempt to deal with the will; two involving a more or less frontal attack, one by a roundabout approach so as to get at it from the rear.

The two frontal attacks are subjective. The more direct of these lies in the attempt to force ourselves to will ourselves to work. The prospects of success along this line are not promising. It sets the will to modify itself, and if the will is weak it is not likely to be more successful in this venture than in any other. The other subjective approach is one that we owe to the advocates of the practice of suggestion and autosuggestion. The procedure here is to tell ourselves, in the most plausible manner we can assume, that we are going to work, if in fact we are not already working. If we only imagine ourselves working with sufficient vividness (so the theory runs) we shall soon find ourselves doing so. Not everyone finds this method efficacious. A difficulty is found by some in the fact that it is they themselves who have to assume the plausible manner and in the fact that it is to themselves that they have to assume it. They find it harder 'really' to imagine themselves working than it is to work.

The underlying principle of the more objective approach here suggested is that implicitly expressed in the opening chapter of this book. Man is an instrument for responding to stimulation in ways which facilitate the attainment of his goals. The will to work is in part, at least, a matter of the appropriate stimuli, a matter for the organization of external conditions. It is in part a matter of *methods* but perhaps is most of all a matter of mobilizing the energies of the propensities in the special interests into which the propensities have been canalized. A few suggestions have been offered. If the general principles have been grasped, other methods will be discovered by the student – and these will be the best of all, because adapted more particularly to his individual needs.

This psychological sermon can conveniently end with a general maxim – a recommendation of a *policy* rather than a *principle*, because policies are less rigid, more flexible, than principles. The maxim is: *that every student should be content to do as well as he can the things he can do best*. Not only be content to do, but *resolve to do* and to *make an effort to do* as well as he can the things he can do best.

There are, of course, ultimate individual differences in the energies and abilities of men. Throughout this study we have been concerned with efficiency of function as a resultant of motivation and of method. But when all is said and done there *are* individual differences in innate endowment. We do, of course, differ in our inborn powers; but let this not become an inhibiting idea or an over-weening obsession. Excluding the extremes of stark mental deficiency and of genius, the differences between most of us largely boil down to the difference in speed – in the time we take to grasp a point. Those fortunately endowed may see it at a glance. The rest of us must take our time; but with method and adequate motivation we may see it in the end.

We may take comfort in the fact that if mental tests are applied at the gates of Heaven they will not be the tests of our innate capacities. If the parable of the talents may be trusted, they will be tests of the use that we have made of them. And this is a common test imposed in mundane life as well.

Further Reading

PERHAPS the reader should be advised not to read anything more, for the time being, on the psychology of study but to get back to his studies – in science, languages, philosophy, or whatever those studies may be. However, he has been advised in the text to check one exposition against another. There are two other books easily accessible which have been written mainly with the British educational system in mind (there are many other good books less accessible and geared to other educational systems). The two books are both published under the same title: *How to Study*. Michael Guinery's book (Allen & Unwin) is by a writer experienced in teaching pupils ranging in age from eleven to twenty-five. The book by Harry Maddox (Pan Books) is by an educational psychologist who holds a post in the very subject of Methods of Study. Both these books cover in detail many topics dealt with only briefly in the *Psychology of Study*. There is another book, in fact *two* other books which deal in more detail and more professionally with an important subject which has been squeezed out of this brief *Psychology of Study* – the emotional problems of students. They are Dr Clifford Allen's *Passing Examinations* (Macmillan 1963) and *Passing School Examinations* (Macmillan 1964), which latter is largely concerned with the anxieties of parents. Dr Allen is both a neuro-psychiatrist and a novelist. He knows much and can say what he knows. His books are good reading.

The *Psychology of Study*, though written for all students, is perhaps slanted a little towards the interests of students of psychology itself and others who may wish to become students of psychology. The following notes accordingly refer to further reading for such students.

Chapter 1 was intended as a very small thumb-nail sketch of what psychology is about. The title was facetious – so much so that one reviewer who did not see the joke intended describes it as pretentious. It was and remains inadequate as an introduction to psychology. Those who want to know more might do worse than begin with one or both of the two Pelicans: C. J. Adcock's *Fundamentals of Psychology* and Peter McKellar's *Experience and Behaviour* (to be published early in 1968).

Chapter 2 could well be followed up by reading M. D. Vernon's Pelican: *The Psychology of Perception.*

Chapter 3: There is no better general introduction to the theory of memory than Ian Hunter's Pelican on *Memory.*

Chapter 4: For more about Thinking, see Robert Thomson's *The Psychology of Thinking.* A rather more advanced but very lively text is *Thinking about Thinking* by Joan Wynn Reeves (Secker and Warburg).

Chapter 5: There is no single book which covers the whole theory of motivation. Indeed more than half of contemporary writings in psychology today concern this subject – especially if one includes, as one must, the writings of psycho-analytic writers and those who are critical of the psycho-analytic approach. In the Pelicans alone there are many useful texts in which both the pros and cons are well represented.

But the reader who proposes to embark on a systematic study of Psychology should be warned: he cannot expect to be told the whole truth and the final truth as he can expect to be told the final (or all but final) truth in other scientific subjects. Psychology remains a very controversial study – a subject with 'schools of thought' and diverse approaches. He *can* expect to be introduced to a number of very exciting hypotheses (i.e. plausible guesses) which psychologists are trying their best to verify. In this he must pull his weight – to attempt to clarify and to verify, to exercise his own judgement.

Index